STUDENT UNIT G

A2 Physical Education
UNIT 6(B)

Edexcel

Section B: Sports Psychology

Matt Stevens

Dedicated to Jim Gleeson

Philip Allan Updates
Market Place
Deddington
Oxfordshire
OX15 0SE

tel: 01869 338652
fax: 01869 337590
e-mail: sales@philipallan.co.uk
www.philipallan.co.uk

ISBN-13: 978-0-86003-947-1
ISBN-10: 0-86003-947-1

This guide has been written specifically to support students preparing for the Edexcel A2 Physical Education Unit 6 examination. The content has been neither approved nor endorsed by Edexcel and remains the sole responsibility of the author.

Printed by MPG Books, Bodmin

Environmental information
The paper on which this title is printed is sourced from managed, sustainable forests.

P00544

Contents

Introduction

About this guide 4
Study skills and revision strategies 5
The day before the test 7
The unit test 7

■ ■ ■

Content Guidance

About this section 10
Learning theories
Associationist theories 11
Cognitive theories 13
Personality
The structure of personality 13
Theories of personality 14
Personality assessments 17
Aggression
Aggression and assertion 19
Categories of aggression 20
Aggression theories 20
Causes of aggression and ways to eliminate it 21
The performer in action
Motivation 22
Self-efficacy 26
Attribution theory 29
Anxiety in sport
Activation 32
Arousal 32
Stress 35
Anxiety 35
The sporting environment
Social facilitation 40
Home-field advantage 42
Leadership 43

■ ■ ■

Questions and Answers

About this section 48
Question 1 49
Question 2 53
Question 3 59
Question 4 64
Question 5 69
Question 6 73

Introduction

About this guide

This guide is written to help you prepare for the Unit 6 examination of the Edexcel Physical Education specification. Unit 6 (Scientific Principles of Exercise and Performance) forms part of the A2 assessment. The specification and unit test are split into three sections. This guide focuses on the Sports Psychology option in Section B. This option is designed to give a basic introduction to some aspects of sports psychology. The examination focuses on the application of theories to sporting scenarios.

This **Introduction** explains how to use the guide, outlines the requirements of the unit, gives suggestions for effective revision and offers advice on approaching the unit test.

The **Content Guidance** section revises the main concepts and themes of the specification. It focuses on the application of the theories within a sporting setting. Links are made with other topics, both within this section and in wider areas of the specification.

The **Questions and Answers** section provides a series of questions in the style of the unit test. Sample answers are given; these are accompanied with examiner's comments to show how the answers could have been improved.

How to use the guide

To use this student guide effectively you should read through this Introduction and familiarise yourself with the skills required for this option. Identify the study skills and revision techniques that you think will be most helpful for you and make a habit of using them. Knowing what examiners are looking for, and practising those skills, will help you to gain marks in the unit test. Refer back to this section periodically to remind yourself of the skills and techniques that might help you.

The Content Guidance section should be used to recap the main points of each topic. It does *not* provide a comprehensive account of the subject. If you find that the information here does not bring a wealth of information flooding back, then you should go back to your original sources (e.g. your class notes) and cover the material again in more depth. The Content Guidance section takes psychological theories and puts them into the context of sport, from the perspective of a performer, coach or sports psychologist.

Read the topics in the guide as you cover them in class. You might find that the order of the topics is different from the order in which you are studying them. Do not worry about this — there is no requirement for the topics to be taught in a particular order. You will find, as you complete the course, that much of the information links together. These links are indicated in the Content Guidance section.

The questions in the last section should provide you with useful practice at recognising (and providing) what the examiner wants.

The specification

It is a good idea to have access to the specification. Your teacher should have a copy, but you can obtain your own copy from the internet. This can be downloaded from the Edexcel website (**www.edexcel.org.uk**).

The specification states that 75% of the marks available are based on knowledge and understanding and 25% on the ability to apply the information in explaining a characteristic of a performance and suggesting strategies to improve it.

The aims of the specification are:

- to develop your ability to appreciate the relationship between theory and practice and to apply theoretical knowledge to develop understanding of practical performance in sport
- to promote the capacity to think critically about the relationships between the different factors influencing performance

The Edexcel specification states that students studying the sports psychology option:

- should be able to understand that all performers are individuals with differing attributes that influence the way they perform
- should explore the social influences of performance and the effect of the environment, and understand the interactional relationship of these variables
- will also study the competitive process of sport and develop an appreciation of the effect of anxiety on performance, subsequently analysing methods used to manage its effects

Examination questions will ask students to apply these psychological principles to the sporting arena.

Study skills and revision strategies

Organising your learning

Preparation for the unit test should take place after every lesson. Have a folder with the different topics clearly labelled. It should contain your class notes, homework exercises that have been marked and returned, handouts, notes that you have made from textbooks, and print-outs from related websites.

If your class notes are not particularly neat, it is a good idea to rewrite them. This is something you should do as soon after the lesson as possible, otherwise you will forget things.

A good folder will form the basis of your revision and mean that, as the exam draws closer, you won't have to spend too much time looking up 'new' information.

It is easy to leave a lesson without having completely understood everything and to think that the exam is a long way off and that you will clarify things closer to the time. Imagine if that happens in just one lesson a week for the first 15 weeks of your A2 course. That's a lot of catching up to do!

Organising revision

Start early! An athlete training for the Olympics does not start training a month before the competition. You will know from your personal exercise programme (PEP) that athletes adapt their training throughout the year, increasing the intensity and duration as required.

You should structure a detailed revision timetable:
- Work out how much time you have available for revision.
- Work out how long to spend not only on each subject, but on each unit within that subject.
- Identify specific topics for each period of revision, so that you do not waste time working out what you are going to revise.

Make sure that you have everything to hand before you start revising — you don't want to have to stop to search for a book or file. Put your revision timetable on view in the house, so that everyone knows when you are revising. This will help to cut down distractions. Turn off your mobile phone!

Getting the most from revision

Be aware of how long you can concentrate effectively and work frequent breaks into your revision time, to suit your personal needs. Take time to work out your most effective method of revision — is it making notes, creating diagrams, making up mnemonics or something else?

Keep your homework assignments and make sure that you understand your teachers' comments. If you are not clear about these, check as soon as the work is returned. When revising, you could redo homework questions in order to work towards perfect answers.

Analyse the effectiveness of your revision. Test yourself frequently to find your strengths and the areas that you still need to develop. This will also highlight the most effective revision techniques that you have used.

Watch sport and play sport. Yes, you can call this revision, but you must be revising as you do it. Candidates trying to achieve A and B grades have to show that they can apply their knowledge. They should be able to analyse a performance, identifying why certain events occur and how they could be changed. For example, you might watch a football match and notice how the crowd influences the referee (social facilitation), or how the young snooker player's game falls apart when he reaches the final (anxiety), and you might be able to suggest strategies that could be used in such cases. In your own activities, you could compare different ways of learning, or consider how different attributions change the way you think about future performances.

The day before the test

Over the last few weeks you should have been working hard at your revision. The day before the test it is important to take time to reward yourself. Schedule a couple of hours to revise during the day, but also go out and do something that you enjoy. This will take your mind off the exam and help you relax. Perhaps go to the gym, go shopping or enjoy nine holes of golf. Try to do something that gets you out of the house and involves some form of activity — even if it is only walking.

Organise your equipment for the next day, making sure that you have everything you need. Take comfort in the knowledge that in less than 24 hours, another exam can be ticked off your list. Recognise that you have revised thoroughly and have good reason to be confident in your performance.

The unit test

First, read the front cover of the exam paper carefully. The Unit 6 test has four parts. You have to answer one question from Section A (Exercise and Energy Systems), one question from either Section B: Option A (Sports Mechanics) or Section B: Option B (Sports Psychology), and one from Section C (Synoptic Analysis). The exam lasts 1 hour 45 minutes and is marked out of 100.

Section A contains two questions, of which you have to answer one.

Section B offers two questions on sports mechanics and two on sports psychology. You have to answer one question from Section B. Be open-minded when you come to this section. You might normally feel more comfortable answering sports mechanics questions. However, it is possible that one of the sports psychology questions focuses on the topic of your investigative study and that you can answer that question very well.

Section C offers four or five essay titles, from which you choose one. The questions from Section A and B are each marked out of 25, while Section C is marked out of 50. Edexcel stresses that this does not mean that you should spend twice the amount of time on Section C as on the other questions. The extra weighting of Section C reflects the significance of being able to analyse a topic using a broad knowledge, taking information from all parts of the course.

In each section, you should spend 5 minutes reading the questions and planning your answer, and 30 minutes writing. Make sure that you read all the questions carefully before you make your choice. If you complete Section A or B in less than 30 minutes, you might be able to use the extra time to develop an argument in Section C. However, do not rush Sections A and B — you have plenty of time.

Option B: Sports Psychology

The two questions comprise sub-sections focused on three or four topics. These may then be further broken down. The following points should help you to perform well in the exam. The final point relates specifically to answering sports psychology questions.

- Be aware of how many marks are available. The usual range is from 2 to 8 marks. If it is a 2-mark question, generally you will need to make two points.
- You can often match the length of your answer to the number of marks available.
- Do not rewrite the question in your answer.
- Be concise.
- If you find that you are short of time, write the main points of your answer as bullet points. It is better to do this than not to answer a question.
- If you are answering a question that requires a long answer, make sure that you keep to the point and do not drift into an irrelevant topic. You cannot be given marks for doing this, even if what you have written is correct — answer the question that has been asked!
- You can use 'define, theory, example' as a guide to answering most questions. Write this at the top of your exam paper as a reminder.
  - **Definitions** — if you cannot remember an exact definition, think about how you would describe what you are talking about to a younger person.
  - **Theories** — you need to be familiar with the theories listed in the specification. When describing a theory, use diagrams or graphs where appropriate, making sure that you label them correctly.
  - **Examples** — you should give examples of the theories in action, in a sporting context. If you neglect to give an example when it is required, you may not be awarded *any* marks, even if you have answered the theory part of the question correctly.

These tips are reinforced in the Questions and Answers section of this book.

The day of the exam

Do not try to revise on the day of the exam. At most, you could look over some cue cards. This should reinforce your knowledge and help you to feel confident and ready to sit the exam.

You may find it relaxing to take a walk. On the morning of the exam, it is a good idea to buy a newspaper (preferably a broadsheet) and read the sports section. This could give you some topical and relevant information that you can use as examples in the exam.

Content Guidance

This section is a guide to the content of **Section B (Option B): Sports Psychology** of **Unit 6: Scientific Principles of Exercise and Performance**. It includes the relevant key facts required by the specification and explains the essential concepts. The main areas covered are:

- Learning theories
- Personality
- Aggression
- The performer in action
- Anxiety in sport
- The sporting environment

When answering examination questions, it is essential to demonstrate a good understanding of the definitions and theories covered in this section. You may need to be familiar with the name of the person who developed the theory, the experiments they used to support it, and to be able to give an example of the theory in a sporting context. Just giving examples, without relating the information to a specific theory, is unlikely to earn any marks.

Learning theories

Learning can be defined as a 'relatively permanent change in behaviour due to past experience' (Coon, 1983). You need to be familiar with two schools of thought regarding learning theories:

- associationist theories
- cognitive theories

Associationist theories

Associationist theories are based on a **stimulus–response (S–R) bond**. If the S–R bond is strengthened, then the behaviour is more likely to be repeated in the future. If the bond is weakened or broken, then behaviour is less likely to be repeated.

Thorndike's laws

Thorndike (1898) developed three laws based on the notion that we learn by trial and error:

- **law of effect** — a response will be repeated if pleasure results from the act
- **law of exercise** — a bond between a stimulus and response will become stronger if the behaviour is repeated and weakened if the practice is discontinued
- **law of readiness** — learning can only take place if the learner is physically and mentally able to learn and allowed to do so

Drive (or drive reduction) theory

Hull's (1943) **drive reduction theory** suggests that we have a drive (or need) to learn. As we perform better, our drive to learn the skill is reduced, at least temporarily. The reduction in drive becomes a reinforcer for learning. When the skill can be performed perfectly, the drive to learn is satisfied.

Classical conditioning

Ivan Pavlov (1927) developed **classical conditioning theory** through his work with dogs. He knew that dogs salivated when given food, but found that they could also be 'conditioned' to salivate at the sound of a bell. The dogs would even start to salivate when they were going to be given food — for example, when they saw the feeding bucket or heard the footsteps of someone coming to feed them.

- *Before* conditioning, the sight or taste of food would make the dogs salivate, but the sound of a bell would not. The food is an **unconditioned stimulus (UCS)** and the salivation is an **unconditioned response (UCR)**.
- *During* conditioning, a bell is rung at the same time as the food is presented to the dogs. Since the bell does not naturally initiate salivation, it is called a **neutral**

stimulus (NS): it can only result in salivation if it is combined with an unconditioned stimulus. This stage must be repeated many times for the bell to be a **conditioned stimulus (CS)**.

- *After* conditioning, the dogs will salivate when they hear the bell, thinking that food will follow. At this point, the salivation is called a **conditioned response (CR)**, since it is a consequence of the conditioned stimulus — the bell.

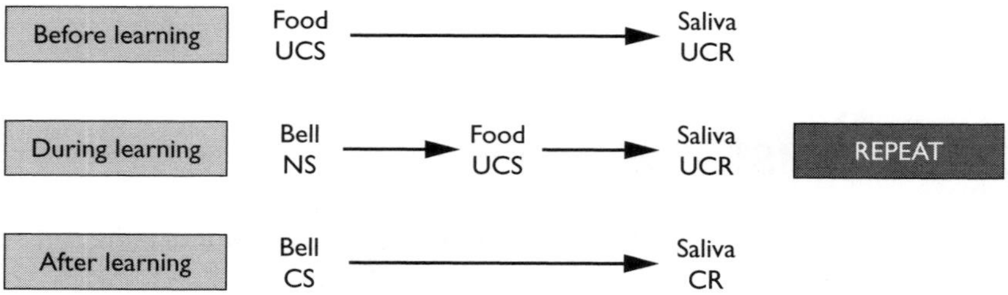

Classical conditioning can also be used in sport. For example, an American footballer found that he focused on irrelevant cues before the start of play. If he told himself to 'focus', he did concentrate on the relevant cues. However, he sometimes forgot to use this verbal cue. Before each play he adjusted his thigh pads. Combining the neutral stimulus of adjusting the thigh pads with the unconditioned stimulus (the verbal cue 'focus'), and repeating this many times, resulted in the adjustment of the thigh pads becoming the conditioned stimulus to concentrate on the relevant cues — the conditioned response.

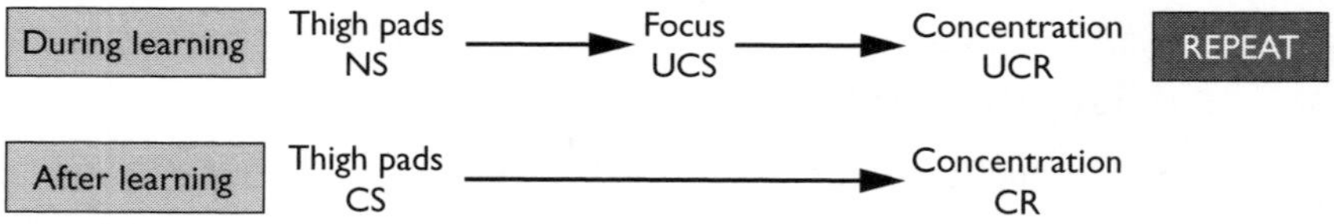

Operant conditioning

Skinner (1938) extended Thorndike's work on learning through trial and error. His **operant conditioning** theory suggests that behaviour is shaped and maintained by its consequences. The consequences can be:

- **positive reinforcement** — presentation of a pleasurable stimulus to promote repetition of the behaviour (e.g. praising a good decision or a skill performed well)
- **negative reinforcement** — removing or avoiding a stimulus to weaken the bond (e.g. substituting a player who is not following the tactics prescribed by the manager)
- **punishment** — presenting a new stimulus to weaken the stimulus–response bond (e.g. a punishment run for a player who fails to work within the team's tactics)

Skinner experimented with rats in a box with a lever. When they bumped into the lever and food was presented (positive reinforcement) the S–R bond was strengthened and the rat repeated the behaviour. When pressing the lever initiated an electric shock (punishment), the S–R bond was weakened and the behaviour was not repeated.

Skinner also experimented on pigeons, and was responsible for the famous video footage of pigeons 'playing' table tennis. In the learning stage, when a pigeon headed the table-tennis ball, it was given a reward. This was repeated with two pigeons, which were eventually able to head the ball to each other.

In PE and sport, operant conditioning takes place all the time. Coaches and teachers attempt to shape the behaviour of their students and players and then give reinforcement. This might be as simple as praising someone's positioning on a basketball court, but that positive reinforcement will increase the chances of the behaviour being repeated in a similar situation in the future. Likewise, giving a negative stimulus or no stimulus should serve to weaken the S–R bond and reduce the chance of the behaviour being repeated.

Cognitive theories

The Gestalt school

The Gestalt school of thinking suggests that we learn by insight — having an understanding of a problem and working out the solution. Researchers such as Koffka, Koehler and Lewin believed that learning through this method would lead to greater understanding and better performance.

Koehler (1925) demonstrated the theory by suspending bananas high above a chimpanzee at the top of the cage. Scattered around the cage were objects that could be used to try to reach the bananas, such as sticks of different lengths (none of which was long enough to reach the bananas) and a number of boxes. Eventually, the chimpanzee solved the problem by stacking the boxes on top of each other and climbing up until he could reach the prize.

In sport, performers with a sound understanding of the fundamental skills are often better able to make good decisions, as opposed to some performers who can perform certain skills very well but often make wrong decisions. This shows the importance of being able to analyse a problem and work out the best solution.

Personality

The structure of personality

Hollander defined personality as the sum of the characteristics that make an individual unique. He suggested that personality has three layers — the psychological core, the middle (typical response) layer and the outer (role-related behaviours) layer:

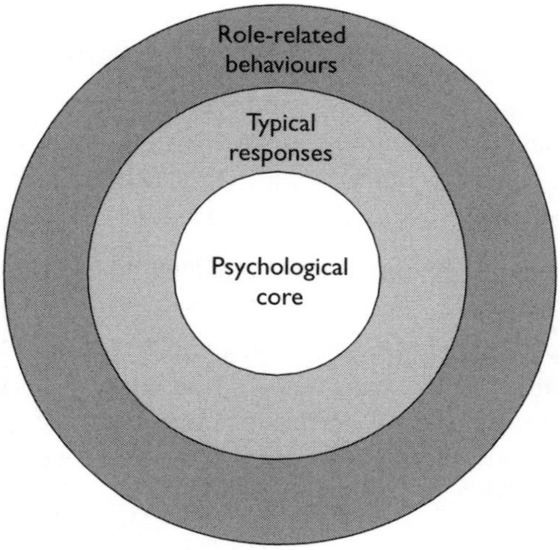

- **Psychological core** — the central component of personality that we rarely allow others to see. Who knows the real you? It is made up of the basic values and attitudes that remain relatively constant and that influence our typical responses. For example, a strong belief about killing animals might influence our typical response about eating meat.
- **Typical responses** — the ways in which people usually respond to situations. It is closely linked with the attitudes and values of the psychological core. For example, if a hockey player believes that there is never an excuse for violence, then he or she is unlikely to behave in a violent fashion.
- **Role-related behaviours** — people respond in ways that they think will best meet the demands of the situation. This might bear little resemblance to the psychological core. For example, although our hockey player believes that there is never an excuse for violence, he or she might hit an opponent's legs with their stick if that is the only way to stop the player scoring.

Zimbardo conducted an experiment in which students adopted the roles of prisoners or prison guards. Within hours, their behaviour changed to match the perceived needs of the situation. More details of the study can be found at **www.prisonexp.org**.

There are many examples in sport of people who exhibit different personalities during a game compared with when they are not playing sport. For example, David Beckham appears quiet and placid off the pitch, but during games he has sometimes reacted in ways that are inconsistent with his typical responses.

Theories of personality

There are a number of different theories to explain how our personalities are developed, and how they influence our interactions with others and the way we deal with situations.

Psychoanalytic theory

Sigmund Freud believed that much of our behaviour is determined by unconscious thoughts, wishes and memories. He suggested that there are three components to personality — the **id**, the **ego** and the **superego**. The id consists of the inherited drives or instincts that seek pleasure. The ego is the part of the personality that contains rationale and logic, enabling us to distinguish between a desire and reality (the id cannot do this). The superego represents the ideal self — the person we want to be. This is dictated by moral values.

There are limitations to the use of psychoanalytic theory in sports psychology. The unconscious aspect of the theory makes it difficult to understand what causes a certain effect and it cannot predict future behaviour. Research in this area is usually based on case studies, so generalisations can be difficult to make.

Humanistic theory

Humanistic theory focuses on the development of the whole person. The theory proposes that an individual's self-perception and self-esteem, related to three key environments, lead us to behave in certain ways (Fox, 1988). These environments are academic, social and physical.

Maslow's **hierarchy of human needs** is a humanistic theory. This hierarchy suggests that we need to satisfy the needs of one level before we can satisfy the needs of the next.

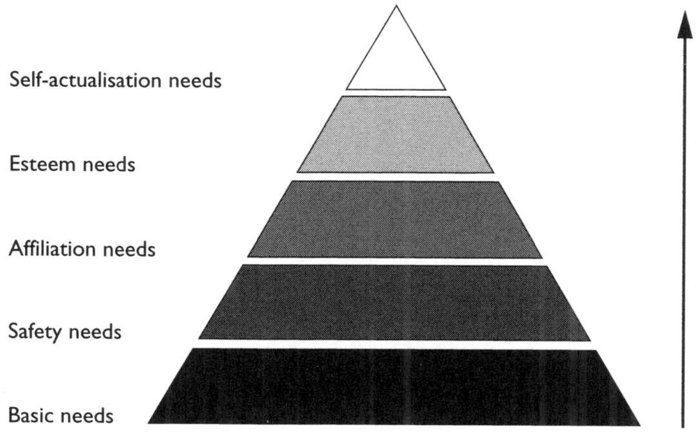

We are motivated towards self-actualisation. At this point, we achieve our ideal selves — we can then be content or we can set future goals. Kelly Holmes 'self-actualised' when she won two gold medals at the Athens Olympic Games. She felt that she could achieve nothing greater in athletics and retired soon afterwards. If she had been younger when she achieved this 'self-actualisation', she might have set further goals, such as breaking the 800 m world record.

Trait theory

This theory suggests that our personality is made up of a series of traits. A trait is a 'general, underlying, enduring predisposition to behave in a particular way each time a given situation occurs'. This means that we will behave consistently throughout our lives, regardless of the situation. Trait theorists claim that we inherit our traits from our parents. The theory is attractive to researchers because traits can be measured easily. It allows people to be classified into certain groups, and predictions of future behaviour can be made. Examples of traits are sensitivity, shyness, motivation, confidence and openness to change.

Early sports psychology research into personality theories attempted to match certain traits with certain sports. This led to some American sports teams giving personality questionnaires to prospective players before drafting them. For example, in ice hockey, motivation, confidence and aggression might be desirable traits. However, the theory does not take into account the influence of the environment or significant others on the development of personality and behaviour.

Eysenck (1967) identified two broad trait dimensions: **extroversion** and **neuroticism**. At one end of the extroversion scale, **extroverts** are outgoing, sociable, confident characters. At the other end, **introverts** tend to be quiet, shy characters who keep themselves to themselves. At one end of the neuroticism scale there are emotionally **stable** individuals, whose behaviour is relatively consistent. At the other end, **neurotic** (or unstable) individuals are often anxious and tense, and experience emotional swings.

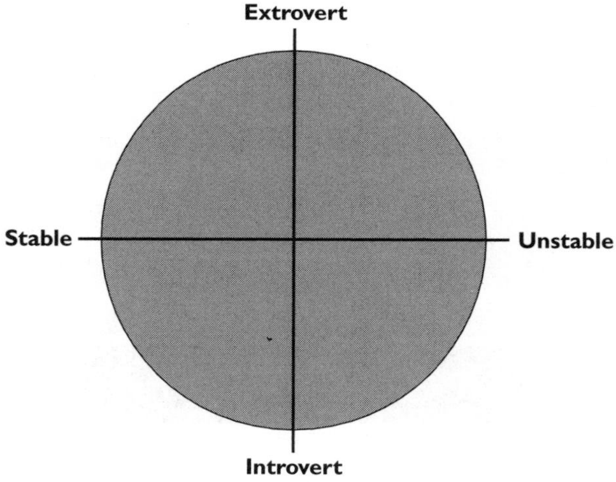

It is a good idea to think of examples to represent the different personality types. For example, Roger Federer is probably a **stable introvert**. If you need to describe the characteristics of a stable introvert, think of Roger Federer and describe his personality. This method is also good for illustrating the weaknesses of the trait approach. Roger Federer's personality make-up is very different from those of Andre Agassi and

John McEnroe, yet they have all been champions in the same sport. Try comparing Wayne Rooney and Michael Owen, who play in the same position but have very different personalities. This shows that there are limitations to matching personalities with sports and with positions in teams.

Social learning theory

Albert Bandura's theory suggests that personality is developed through relationships with others. Bandura (1971) conducted experiments that showed that we model our actions on the behaviour of significant others. This takes place with no deliberate effort from the learner or the teacher. The way in which this behaviour is then reinforced dictates whether or not we are likely to adopt it in the future. This suggests that, regardless of our trait disposition, our behaviour and personality can be developed, based on the people around us.

Tip In answering an exam question on social learning theory, you must include the key words 'modelling' and 'reinforcement'.

In sport, we often model ourselves on sporting heroes by copying their moves or maybe wearing similar clothes. If this behaviour is positively reinforced, we continue to adopt it. If the behaviour is not positively reinforced or if it is punished, we will be less likely to repeat the behaviour.

A limitation of social learning theory is that it does not take into account genetically inherited traits.

Interactionism

Interactionists believe that behaviour (B) is a function (f) of the personality (P) and the environment (E). This can be represented by the formula:

$$B = f(P, E)$$

This theory takes into account the influence of inherited traits and also allows for the influence of other people and of the situation. So, although our traits are consistent, our behaviour changes depending on where we are, whom we are with and what the situation demands from us.

The most recent research suggests that personality is developed through a combination of inherited traits and what we learn from others. It is thought that the ratio is about 60:40, with inherited traits responsible for the larger share.

Personality assessment

There are four common techniques for personality assessment in psychology:
- questionnaires
- interviews

- observation
- psychometric measures, such as the ink-blot test

In sports psychology, it is the first three that are commonly used — you need to know the pros and cons of each of these.

Questionnaires

Commonly used personality questionnaires are:

- Cattell's 16PF questionnaire, which records personality in five global dimensions and 16 first-order dimensions
- the Eysenck personality questionnaire (EPQ), which measures extroversion and neuroticism

Positive points about questionnaires

- They are easy to use.
- They are normally quick to complete.
- Large amounts of data can be collected.
- They are easy to replicate, ensuring that everyone answers the same questions.
- It is easy to obtain quantitative data for analysis.
- Normative data are often available.

Negative points about questionnaires

- Validity issues, i.e. does the questionnaire actually measure what it is being used to measure?
- Reliability issues:
  - People might not tell the truth.
  - People might enter socially desirable answers.
  - Issues might not be investigated in depth.
  - The normative data may not represent the sample population, which might, for example, be culturally specific to the place of origin.

Interviews

Interviews can be structured in a closed or open-ended way to meet the needs of the researcher.

Positive points about interviews

- They allow topics to be covered fully.
- Participants can clarify a question if they are unsure of its meaning.
- Non-verbal communication can reveal if the interviewee is lying.
- They can provide both qualitative and quantitative data.
- Questions can be open-ended. This allows the interviewer to lead the interview in a particular direction.

Negative points about interviews

- They are time consuming and may be difficult to transcribe.
- It is difficult to compare data from different individuals.

- People might give socially desirable answers.
- Questions can be misunderstood and answers can be misinterpreted.
- People might not tell the truth.
- There are no normative data.

Observation

A factor that would influence the pros and cons of observation would be whether or not people knew they were being observed.

Positive points about observation

- Behaviour can be observed in a real environment.
- It can provide both qualitative and quantitative data.

Negative points about observation

- Behaviour is often altered if people know that they are being observed.
- It is difficult to compare data from different individuals.
- Gathering data can be time consuming.
- There are no normative data.

Aggression

An exam question on the topic of aggression will usually ask for a distinction between aggression and assertion. It will ask about one or more of the aggression theories and will ask you to suggest ways to eliminate or reduce the likelihood of aggressive behaviour in sport. You might also be asked to identify common causes of aggression in sport.

Aggression and assertion

Aggression was defined by Baron (1977) as 'any behaviour directed at the goal of harming or injuring another being who is motivated to avoid such treatment'.

The intent to harm can be physical or mental. 'Trash talking' to opponents in an attempt to distract them, to increase anxiety or to reduce their confidence is an aggressive behaviour because there is an attempt to cause mental harm.

Where there is no intent to harm, the behaviour is said to be **assertive**. This is when a player plays at a high intensity, usually with high arousal, but within the rules. For example, a basketball player might drive past a defender and dunk, or a footballer might commit fully to a 50:50 tackle. Confusion in sport occurs when players, coaches or commentators describe these actions as aggressive play, when the psychological definition suggests that they are examples of assertive play. Unfortunately, the word 'assertion' does not carry the same emotion as the word 'aggression', so the latter is used more frequently.

Categories of aggression

Hostile aggression

Hostile aggression is when the primary aim of the action is to cause harm. This form of aggression is against the rules in sport. Even in boxing, the primary aim is to score points or to prevent the opponent from continuing — not to cause harm.

Instrumental aggression

Instrumental aggression is an action that has a different goal, but where harm might be a by-product. For example, a footballer might raise his arms to help him to jump higher, knowing that his elbow might catch an opponent in the face. Another example is a tennis player smashing a ball directly at the opponent. This is done to make the ball more difficult to return. However, if the ball hits the opponent, he or she could be injured.

Aggression theories

Ethological approaches (instinct)

These theories suggest that aggression is a natural instinct. Freud suggested that we are born with a self-destructive force to be aggressive. Lorenz suggested that humans have the same aggressive instinct as animals — to defend territory and fight for survival. Ethologists also believe that aggression builds up in people until it reaches such a point that it has to be released and expressed. Sport is seen as a way of 'letting-off steam' and releasing the aggression.

Research has shown that humans are able to use reason and logic to control their aggressive instincts. Hence, these theories lack support.

Trait and social learning theories

Trait theorists propose that we have an aggressive trait that is naturally higher in some people than others.

Bandura demonstrated his social learning theory through aggressive acts. He found that children who observed their parents acting aggressively by hitting 'bobo' dolls modelled their behaviour on their parents. The way this behaviour was reinforced influenced whether or not the children repeated the action. An example of this in sport can be taken from football. When David Beckham was a young player at Manchester United, he greatly admired Eric Cantona. In the 1998 World Cup finals, when Beckham was sent off for kicking Simeone, was his behaviour modelled on that of Cantona? (Eric Cantona had been banned by the FA for 9 months for kicking a Crystal Palace fan.) On his return, Manchester United made him captain. What sort of reinforcement was this, and what message did it send to the young players at Manchester United? Social learning theory could be used to suggest that these actions are linked.

Drive theory (the frustration–aggression hypothesis)

Within their drive theory, Dollard et al. (1939) suggested the hypothesis that aggression will result from frustration caused by not being able to achieve a goal. There are limitations to this theory, since aggressive behaviour does not *always* follow such frustration.

Aggressive cue theory (a revised frustration–aggression hypothesis)

Berkowitz (1996) recognised the limitation of the frustration–aggression hypothesis and suggested that when a goal is blocked, frustration increases, as does the *likelihood* of aggressive behaviour through increasing anger and arousal. However, this does not always lead to an aggressive act. Berkowitz argued that increased arousal and anger will lead to aggressive behaviour if **socially learnt cues** suggest that aggression is an appropriate response. However, if the cues suggest that aggression is inappropriate, then it will not occur. For example, in ice hockey, aggressive behaviour is frequently given positive reinforcement. Therefore, when a player is frustrated, aggression often occurs. In basketball, aggressive behaviour is negatively reinforced. Therefore, a basketball player is less likely to act aggressively, even though he/she might be feeling the same level of frustration as the ice hockey player.

Causes of aggression and ways to eliminate it

What causes aggression in sport?

When the activity or game increases arousal more than is usual — such as when competing in a final or an important competition — the likelihood of aggression is increased. Aggression is also more likely when a player is:

- losing
- perceiving unfair officiating
- embarrassed, injured or in pain
- playing below capabilities
- reacting to something perceived as deliberate
- playing away from home

- performing in front of others (social facilitation/evaluation apprehension)
- encouraged by the coach to be aggressive

How can we eliminate aggression?

Berkowitz's theory explains how frustration can lead to aggression and Bandura's theory explains how we model ourselves on significant others. Based on these theories, we can create a list of interventions to control arousal and frustration, to punish aggressive actions and to reinforce non-aggressive behaviour. These might include:

- fair-play awards
- reinforcing positive role models in the media
- society (especially schools) highlighting non-aggressive role models
- reducing the publicity given to aggressive behaviour
- severe punishments for aggressive behaviour
- involving the law courts to punish aggressive behaviour
- using sports psychologists for support and guidance
- professional officiating
- coaches differentiating between aggression and assertion

The performer in action

Motivation

Motivation was defined by Sage (1977) as 'the internal mechanisms and external stimuli that arouse and direct behaviour'.

Achievement motivation theory

Achievement motivation theory identifies two personality types. Some people are driven by a **need to achieve** (**nAch**), while others **need to avoid failure** (**naF**). People with a high need to achieve like to be challenged and persist even when the situation is difficult. They are not motivated by easy tasks. People with a high need to avoid failure will only take part in very easy tasks at which they cannot fail or very difficult tasks at which they cannot succeed. They do not want to face the shame and humiliation associated with losing. If the task is very easy, they will succeed; if the task is very difficult, they have reason for failing before they start.

It is important to remember that these personality types are independent of each other. This means that it is possible for a person to be high in need to achieve *and* high in need to avoid failure. The graph below illustrates the extremes of the personality types.

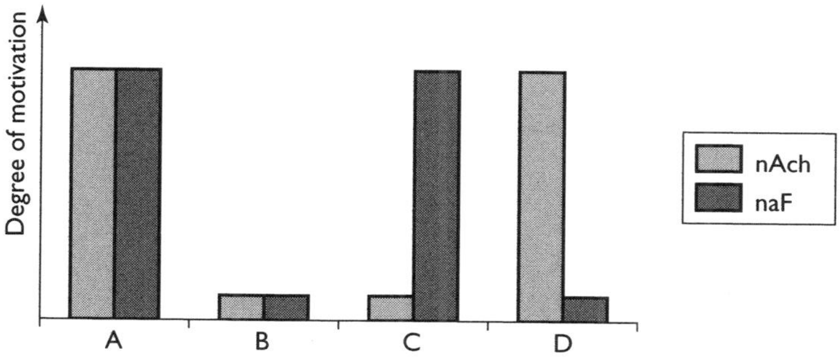

Terry (1997)

Personality A (high nAch, high naF) — People in this group enjoy competition and take responsibility for outcomes. However, failure will cause self-doubt and could lower self-esteem. They might resort to poor sportsmanship in an attempt not to fail, and will not persist for long when things become difficult. These traits are evident in many sportspeople who fail to achieve their potential.

Personality B (low nAch, low naF) — People in this group are not motivated to take part in competition. They are very laid back and lack ambition.

Personality C (low nAch, high naF) — People in this group avoid competition if there is any chance of being beaten. They might take part if they are guaranteed to win — for example, if they were to play one-on-one basketball against a 5 year old.

Personality D (high nAch, low naF) — This is the best profile for a sportsperson. People in this group love the challenge of competition, especially when the task is difficult and the outcome uncertain. They love to win, because they have to overcome a difficult challenge, but know that losing is a part of competition and they use defeats as learning experiences. They are very persistent and have high self-motivation.

Self-motivation

As stated in the definition above, motivation can be internal or external. Examples of intrinsic motivators include:

- enjoyment
- pride
- feeling good
- looking good
- being the best
- proving others wrong
- mastering a task

Examples of extrinsic motivators include:

- praise
- money

- trophies
- fame
- publicity
- titles
- sponsorship

There is considerable evidence that intrinsic motivation is stronger and more enduring than extrinsic motivation. Think about all the top sportspeople who have amassed enough wealth never to have to work again, yet continue to train hard and strive to win more titles — Venus Williams, Michael Schumacher and David Beckham, for example. Michael Jordan retired after winning three NBA titles. Two years later he came back to win three more titles before again retiring. He returned to the NBA 2 years later and finally retired at the age of 40.

Extrinsic motivators can enhance motivation for a while, but eventually lose value. They can actually decrease motivation, because people get used to being given a reward and when the reward is no longer available, they do not want to perform the desired behaviour.

Observational learning

Motivation is an important part of learning. Bandura described how we learn by watching others. His diagram of **observational learning** shows the process. We watch someone's behaviour, paying attention to what is done and how it is done. We then remember this information and, if motivated sufficiently, attempt to copy the behaviour, resulting in a model of the original demonstration.

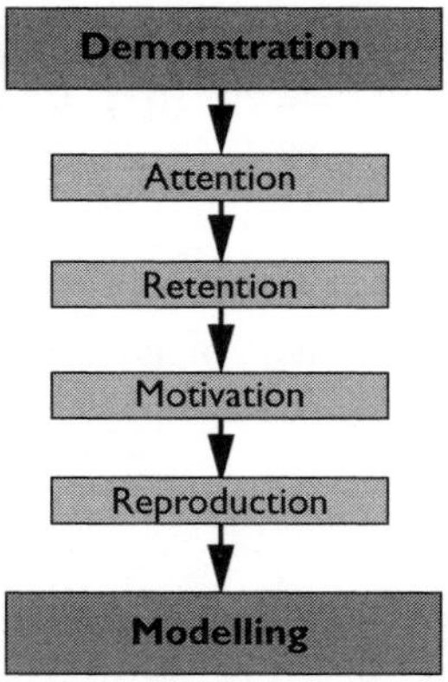

We often see people attempting to re-create skills and tricks performed by some of the world's best footballers. Recent television commercials have shown Roberto Carlos, Ronaldo, Zinedine Zidane, David Beckham and Thierry Henry performing skills. Bandura's model illustrates how people might watch the trick performed and remember how the player executed it. They might then be motivated to practise the trick repeatedly, so that they can be like the player in the commercial. The ability to be able to reproduce a model of the trick successfully in front of others would bring positive reinforcement.

In PE and sport, teachers need to make sure that a demonstration is accurate. A poor demonstration will lead to poor models. It must also be memorable. If the demonstration is too complex or too fast, the learner may not retain the information.

How to measure motivation

As with personality, motivation can be measured by a questionnaire, interview or observation. The easiest method to use on a large scale is a questionnaire. Validated questionnaires are available to identify motivation orientation (nAch or naF, ego-orientated or task-orientated) or self-motivation.

One such questionnaire, the Self-Motivation Inventory (SMI), has been validated for use with adult athletes and with children. This is scored on a scale from 1 (No — extremely uncharacteristic of me) to 5 (Yes — extremely characteristic of me). Examples of the items are:

- I work harder than most of my friends.
- It takes a lot to get me going.
- I really want to achieve things.
- If something becomes too much of an effort, I am likely to stop doing it.

How to increase motivation

Goal setting

Goal setting is aimed at increasing intrinsic motivation. Goals serve to direct attention and mobilise energy. When setting goals, we should follow the '**smarter**' guidelines. Goals must be:

- **s**pecific
- **m**easurable
- **a**greed
- **r**ealistic
- **t**ime-phased
- **e**xciting
- **r**ecorded

If a goal is not **specific** (for example, to do better...), the performer will not know exactly what to work on or if improvement is being made. A goal must be **measurable** so that the performer can monitor progress. Many goals can be compared with statistics. If this is not possible, performers can award themselves marks out of 10 in the particular skill, with 10 marks being the perfect model. Goals need to be **agreed** between the performer and the coach or teacher. A goal set by the player alone might not be in line with the plans of the coach. However, a goal set by the coach, without agreement from the performer, might be working towards something that does not interest the performer. Therefore, the performer might not be motivated to work towards it. If a goal is not **realistic**, the performer will soon realise that it cannot be achieved and will lose motivation and withdraw from the activity. Goals need to be **time-phased**, with short-term goals leading to mid-term goals, which in turn lead to long-term goals. They need to be **exciting** or challenging. An easy goal will not motivate a performer, since there is nothing to prove by achieving it and the individual's self-esteem will not be enhanced. Finally, goals need to be **recorded**. We have ups and downs in sport and in life — it is good to be able to look back periodically and see what we have achieved.

Rewards

Rewards should be small 'tokens', given periodically and without warning. Intrinsic motivation is more valuable than extrinsic motivation, so a teacher or coach needs to ensure that rewards do not become a distraction or become perceived as more important than any intrinsic motivator.

Self-efficacy

Any question on self-efficacy will ask you about Bandura's theory and will want you to apply your knowledge by giving a sporting example. You might also have to suggest how to enhance self-efficacy.

Bandura's self-efficacy theory

Self-efficacy was defined by Bandura (1977) as 'self-confidence in any given situation'.

In other words, it is a situation-specific confidence and is different from the global self-confidence construct. For example, a person might be very confident generally, but might have low self-efficacy for being able to ski a difficult black run without stopping. On the other hand, a person with low self-confidence might have high self-efficacy for shooting in netball.

Bandura suggested that there are four 'antecedents' or sources of self-efficacy and that these are hierarchical. The most important is **performance accomplishments**, followed by **vicarious experiences**, then **verbal persuasion** and finally **control of emotional arousal**.

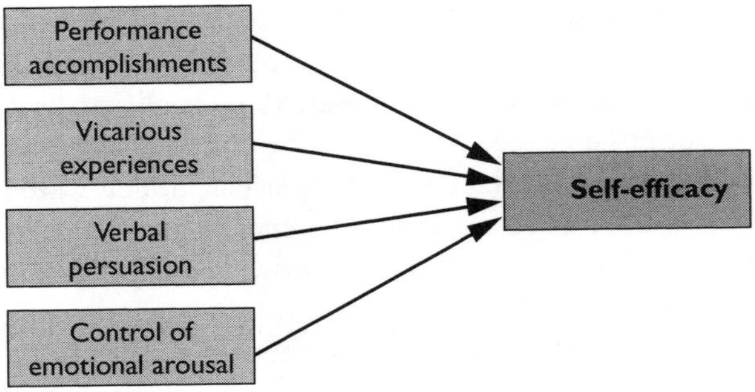

Performance accomplishments

If performers have previously achieved success, they will have high self-efficacy for doing it again. For example, if a swimmer has achieved a sub-30-second time in a 50-metre freestyle race, the belief will be there that this can be repeated in the future.

Vicarious experiences

If someone has achieved a goal, then people will know that it is possible, even if they have not achieved the goal themselves. For example, before 6 May 1954, no-one had run a mile in under 4 minutes despite many years of trying. People were beginning to think it might not be possible and some physiologists thought it would endanger the health of any athlete who attempted it. However, once Roger Bannister broke the 4-minute barrier, people knew that it was indeed possible and self-efficacy increased through this vicarious experience. Within 46 days, another athlete had broken the barrier and by the end of 1957, 16 individuals had achieved the goal.

Verbal persuasion

The effectiveness of verbal persuasion in increasing self-efficacy is influenced by the perceived status of the person and the method of delivery. For example, a young sprinter who is told by Linford Christie that he *can* run 100 metres in under 11 seconds will hold more value in the words of a former champion and respected coach than if he were told the same thing by his grandmother.

The way the message is put across is also important. This can be:

- one-to-one or public
- emotional or logical
- subtle or confrontational

The intelligence, self-esteem and personality characteristics of the performer need to be considered as well. To be truly effective, the message needs to be tailored to the individual.

Control of emotional arousal

In sporting situations, this is often linked with controlling negative emotions, such as anxiety. Generally, when people are experiencing high-level anxiety, they have low self-efficacy for the task. Performers should have a rehearsed strategy, or series of strategies, to help control such negative emotions. Sometimes performers are under-aroused for a performance. This too can lead to lower self-efficacy. Again, a well-prepared athlete or coach would have a plan to overcome such a problem.

The effects of high self-efficacy on behaviour

Certain benefits are associated with having high self-efficacy prior to and during a performance. These include:

- positive emotions:
  - remaining calm
  - performing with composure even when things are difficult
  - being assertive

- good concentration (not being distracted)
- setting challenging goals rather than easy goals
- high levels of effort
- good persistence under difficult circumstances
- positive playing strategies:
  - playing to win rather than not to lose
  - taking more risks
- generating momentum:
  - evidence of game-to-game momentum
  - being able to control momentum in a game
  - being able to win after falling behind

If you have to answer an exam question about how self-efficacy influences performance, rather than attempting to repeat this list, think of a successful team or person in your sport and describe how self-efficacy helps them. You will probably find that many of the factors you pick out are in the list above. However, by making your answer personal and referring to a person or team with whom you are familiar, you will find these easier to remember.

Consequences of high self-efficacy

High self-efficacy is generally considered to have a positive linear relationship with performance. This means that the higher self-efficacy is, the better the performance. Some people claim that a performer can be over-confident, although the evidence does not support this. However, sometimes people who have very high self-efficacy can be complacent and prepare poorly or make poor decisions.

Strategies for enhancing self-efficacy

Strategies need to be focused on the theory and the antecedents of self-efficacy (see page 26). These antecedents are hierarchical, and so should be prioritised.

Performance accomplishments

These strategies focus on what the individual has achieved in the past. If the individual has successfully completed the upcoming task (or an equal task) on a previous occasion, reminders of this should be given. There might be a video of a previous performance that could be watched. If not, imagery is an excellent substitute. Is there a performance diary or journal that could be revisited? Is there an opportunity to visit the competition site before the day of competition and train or rehearse there? Can a marathon runner walk, drive or even run the course? Imagery can be used to 'project' a performance in the individual's mind. If the performer has not been successful in the task before, the mind will assume success, which will increase self-efficacy.

Vicarious experiences

These strategies focus on the success of others. For example, your team might be facing a particularly good team in a cup final. You haven't played this team before, but you might have beaten a team that has done so in a different competition.

A video of someone else's performance could be used to gain self-efficacy and then imagery could project the individual into the successful performance.

Verbal persuasion

This can be used to reinforce information taken from the two antecedents above. The individual must respect and trust the persuader for it to be effective.

Control of emotional arousal

This strategy focuses on the need of the individual, whether it be increasing arousal, decreasing arousal or reducing anxiety. Imagery or relaxation strategies might be used. Listening to music can be used to psych up, calm down or distract. Having a set routine can help a performer to prepare for a competition and remove uncertainty. Setting short-term, achievable goals, which are focused on mastering tasks or on an individual's performance (not the outcome), can also be used to reduce anxiety and enhance self-efficacy. More strategies are included in the section on anxiety (page 32).

Attribution theory

Attribution is how individuals think about the cause of an outcome — for example, the reason why they won or lost. The way the information is perceived is the important factor. This influences the motivation and self-efficacy of performers and subsequent performances.

Weiner (1979) identified four main categories of attribution:

- ability
- effort
- task difficulty
- luck

Weiner's model identified two dimensions:

- **Stability** refers to how circumstances might change or not change over a period of time (e.g. from game to game).
- **Locus of causality** refers to whether the factor is internal or external. For example, effort is internal and luck is external.

		Locus of causality	
		Internal	External
Stability	Stable	Ability	Task difficulty
	Unstable	Effort	Luck

Weiner (1985) introduced a third dimension — **controllability**. This refers to whether the outcome is within the control of the performer or is controlled by other people.

There are many other factors that can be attributed to an outcome. Some of these are shown in the diagram below.

Locus of causality

Stability	Internal	External
Stable	Playing ability Personality characteristics (trait motivation, anxiety etc.) Training Fitness	Leadership Task difficulty Quality of opponent (if in a league) Coaching Equipment Playing surface (if consistent)
Unstable	Effort Self-efficacy Concentration Communication Arousal level	Luck Quality of opponent Weather Officials Playing surface (if variable)

Some factors can appear in two boxes. For example, the Astroturf® playing surface in field hockey is stable, but there can be vast differences in the quality of football and cricket pitches, which could influence the outcome of a game. Likewise, the quality of opponent could be stable or unstable. A top sprinter will always compete against fellow elite athletes, most of whom, at their best, are capable of running sub-10 seconds. Other sportspeople might face a good opponent one week and a poor opponent another week.

Attribution, emotions and performance

A successful performance should be attributed to internal and/or stable factors — for example: 'we won because we are good players' or 'we won because we showed great effort'. Positive outcomes that are perceived to be internal contribute to feelings of pride and satisfaction. Individuals are motivated to repeat the performance and they have high self-efficacy.

An unsuccessful performance that is attributed to internal or stable factors will decrease motivation and self-efficacy — for example: 'we lost because we aren't good enough' or 'we lost because we aren't fit enough'. Since ability and fitness cannot be quickly improved, the performers will have negative expectations for the next competition. This kind of attribution is associated with feelings of shame and dissatisfaction. Whenever possible, unsuccessful performances should be attributed to external and/or unstable factors — for example: 'we lost because our effort was poor' or 'we lost because we are not used to playing on Astroturf®, while our opponents train on it regularly'. In the first example, the players know that they can increase their effort in the next competition. In the second example, the players know that this was a one-off performance on an all-weather surface and that most games are played on grass. By making external and/or unstable attributions, coaches are trying to protect the motivation and self-efficacy of their athletes.

The attribution process (Carron, 1981)

Albert Carron developed the attribution process model to help us understand how our attribution of an outcome will influence our emotions and motivation to take part in the activity in the future.

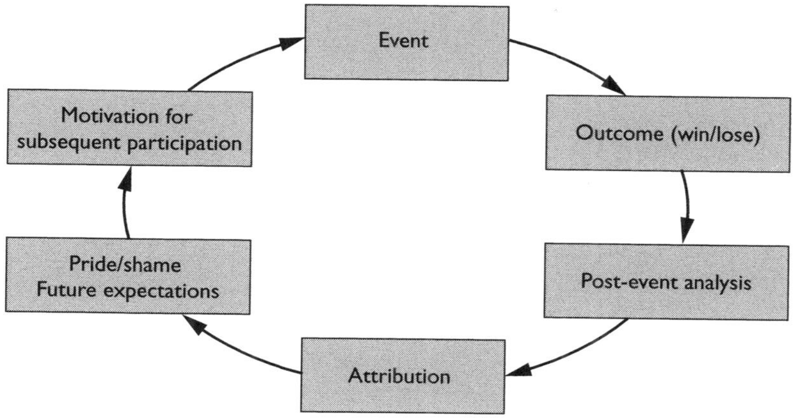

Using attributions for future performances

As shown in Carron's model, analysis and attribution influence future expectations. If successful performances are regularly attributed to ability and work ethic, then, provided we maintain the work ethic, we expect to be successful.

In contrast, some people develop **learned helplessness** by repeatedly attributing poor performances to internal and stable factors or uncontrollable factors. This is often evident in people with low self-esteem. It may lead them to expect to fail before even attempting a task. Learned helplessness from one domain can then spread to other areas of sport and even to life — for example: 'I'm no good at shooting in netball' could lead to 'I'm no good at netball' and then to 'I'm no good at sport'. This could then lead to 'I'm no good at practical things' and 'I'm not an active person'. Setting goals at the correct level and guaranteeing some success can help to avoid learned helplessness.

Self-fulfilling prophecy

The self-fulfilling prophecy is when we expect something to happen and then work to make it happen. This is generated through analysing past experiences and attributions. Sports psychologists often use the phrase 'wysiwyg' (What you see is what you get!). If you truly believe that you will be successful, you probably will be. If you expect to lose, you will lose. For example, a golfer might attribute a high score to poor putting. If this performance is repeated, a point will be reached at which the expectation will be to putt badly. Consequently, the golfer *will* putt badly.

Anxiety in sport

This part of the specification brings together activation, arousal, stress and anxiety. You need to be able to define the different constructs, know how they are related to each other and know how they can influence a performance.

Activation

Activation refers to the **physical** and **mental** state of **readiness**. Physical activation is associated with heart rate, blood pressure, body temperature, adrenaline levels and so on. Mental activation is associated with levels of alertness, focus on attention and perceived importance of the upcoming task.

Arousal

Arousal is a state of general **physiological** and **psychological activation**, ranging in intensity from deep sleep to intense excitement. It is important for athletes to know, and be able to compete at, their optimum arousal level. Being over- or under-aroused can have serious implications for performance.

The inverted-U hypothesis

The inverted-U hypothesis (Yerkes and Dodson, 1908) suggests that as arousal increases, so does performance, up to an optimal point. After this point, as arousal continues to increase, performance decreases.

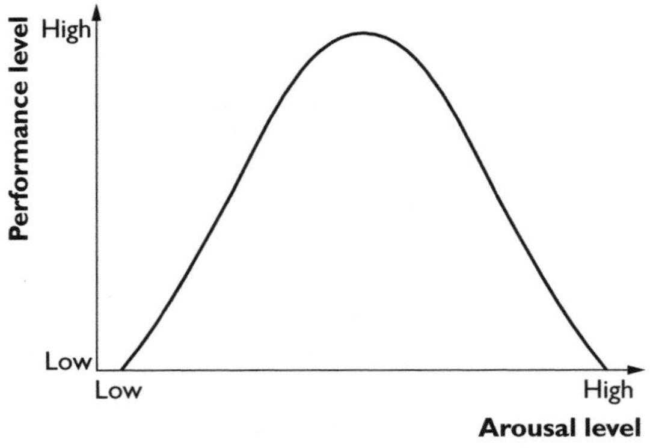

In sport, the relationship between performance and arousal can be influenced by factors such as personality, skill level, type of skill or activity and the presence of others (discussed later).

Tip If you are asked a question related to arousal, try to draw graphs in your answer to illustrate your understanding. Make sure that you label any graphs correctly.

Arousal and skill level

If two people, one in the cognitive stage of learning and one in the autonomous stage, are performing the same task, it is probable that the cognitive learner will experience higher arousal than the autonomous learner, since the situation may be unknown. For the more experienced learner, a higher level of arousal needs to be achieved or boredom could set in, resulting in underperformance. Unskilled or low-skilled performers will probably perform poorly when under pressure because they will be over-aroused. Highly skilled performers will tend to excel when under pressure, when arousal is moderately high.

Arousal for different personality types

Introverts will probably perform at their optimum at a low level of arousal; the optimum level of arousal for an extrovert might be much higher.

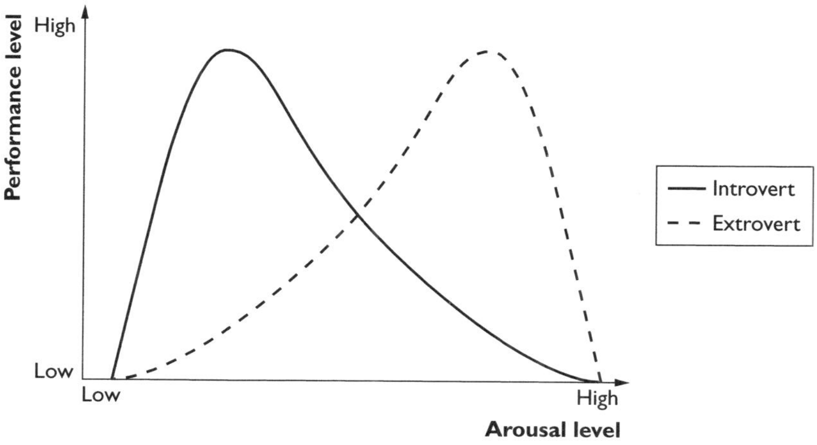

Arousal and type of skill or activity

Activities that involve mainly gross motor skills (e.g. rugby) are associated with higher levels of arousal than activities that involve more fine motor skills (e.g. archery and shooting). In some sports, winning or losing can depend on the ability of the competitors to lower their arousal levels quickly. An example is the biathlon, in which competitors have to ski (gross motor skill) and shoot at targets (fine motor skill). Optimum levels of arousal for fine and gross motor skills are shown in the graph below.

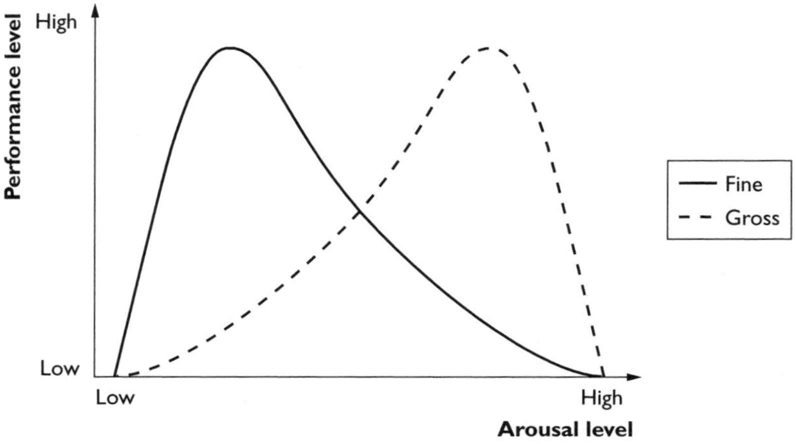

Consequences of low and high arousal

Low arousal

If athletes are under-aroused, they are probably not particularly concerned about the outcome of the competition. Their focus of attention might be too broad, allowing them to be distracted by irrelevant cues or to miss relevant ones. Think of times when you have been sitting in a classroom and missed information that the teacher has given, or times when you have been distracted. This is a consequence of your focus of attention being too broad, or in the wrong direction.

Under-arousal means that the level of activation will also be low. When a cue that requires action *is* recognised, the athlete could react too slowly.

High arousal

Over-arousal can result in a narrowing of attention, which can also lead to performers missing relevant cues. An example of this is when a player is fouled in football and experiences 'red mist'. The player becomes solely focused on the irrelevant cues associated with revenge and the football cues are missed. Being over-aroused can cause misinterpretation of cues even when they are recognised, and very high arousal can cause disorientation. High arousal is also associated with increased muscular tension, which can have a negative effect on performance in some sports and, in certain cases, lead to injury.

Arousal-inducing strategies

Sometimes athletes are under-aroused and instead of having to reduce arousal, they need to induce or increase it. Some of the techniques used for coping with anxiety (see pages 39–40) can be used in this situation, though they might be used slightly differently. These include:

- increasing breathing rate
- listening to music (up-tempo music, with some personal relevance or sporting image, such as the music from *Rocky*, or your rugby team's favourite song)

- association
- imagery of positive, assertive or physical behaviour
- positive self-statements
- a vigorous warm-up

Stress

Stress is a **physiological** and **psychological reaction** to a **stressor**. Stress can be brought on by internal causes (such as trait anxiety or low self-esteem) or external situational factors (such as the importance of the event).

Stress increases arousal, which, depending on the individual's starting and optimum arousal points, could be positive or negative in terms of performance. If the stress produces excitement and raises arousal to the player's optimum level, then it is positive. If the stress distracts the performer and takes arousal beyond the optimum point, then it will have a negative influence on performance. In its negative forms, stress can lead to frustration (and possibly aggression) and anxiety.

The stress process, shown below, illustrates how a situation can lead to a stress response. Generally, some stress is positive, as it increases the level of arousal and activation, but athletes need to be aware of their arousal levels and have planned strategies to reduce, maintain or increase them.

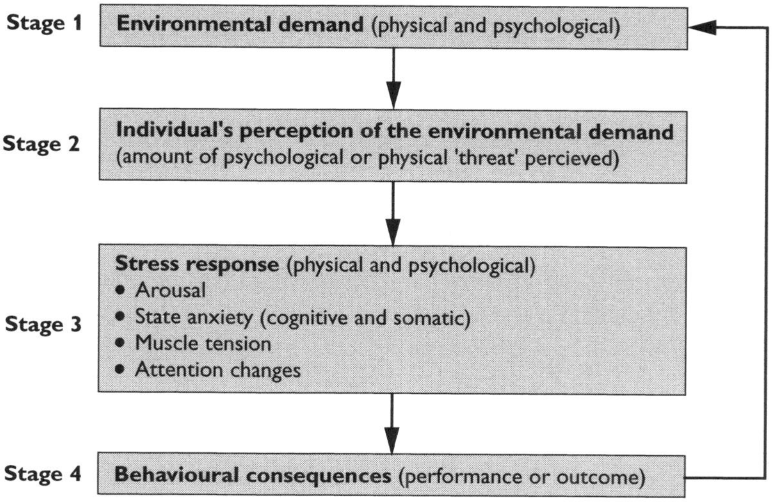

Anxiety

Anxiety is defined by Weinberg and Gould (2003) as 'a negative emotional state with feelings of worry, nervousness and apprehension associated with activation of the body'.

It is caused by a perceived imbalance between the demands of the task and ability. Anxiety is closely linked to stress and arousal, as it is often caused by stress and usually results in an increase in arousal.

Anxiety can be a trait or state construct. Traits are general, underlying, enduring predispositions to behave in a particular way each time a situation occurs. Someone high in trait anxiety will regularly feel anxious in everyday life, often when it is not justified. People who report high levels of trait anxiety usually have more state anxiety than people reporting low trait anxiety, in the same situation.

A state construct is one that is influenced by the situation. It will fluctuate from moment to moment. So, while an individual might not have high trait anxiety, the notion of boxing against Vitali Klitschko might induce high state anxiety.

Competitive state anxiety can be caused by:

- lack of belief in ability
- fear of failure
- fear of making mistakes
- fear of underperforming
- fear of evaluation by others
- fear of the opponent or the event
- fear of injury
- fear of danger associated with the event (e.g. skydiving)
- lack of control over the circumstances

Multidimensional state anxiety

McGrath (1970) suggests that there are two dimensions of anxiety: **cognitive** and **somatic**. Cognitive anxiety is characterised by negative thoughts, while somatic anxiety is characterised by physiological changes, such as sweaty palms, increased heart rate and 'butterflies' in the stomach.

Cognitive anxiety

The multidimensional state anxiety theory proposes that cognitive anxiety has a negative linear relationship with performance — the more negative thoughts we have, the worse we perform. This seems logical, since if we are thinking about how bad we are, we cannot be attending to the relevant cues. The relationship between cognitive anxiety and performance is shown in the graph below.

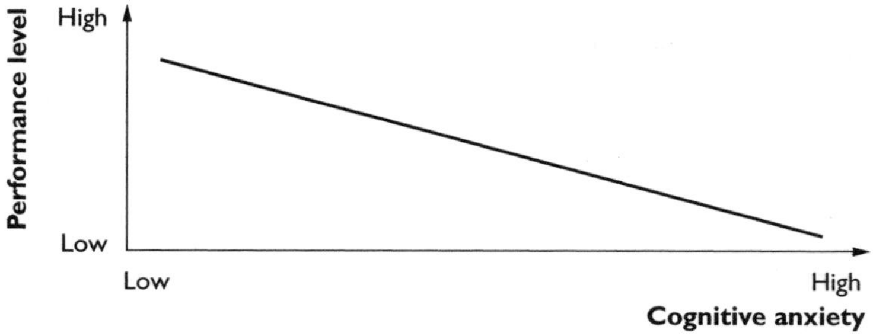

Symptoms of cognitive anxiety include:

- narrowing of the focus of attention
- poor concentration
- self-centred thoughts
- negative thoughts about ability
- worrying about failure
- inability to make decisions, often for fear of being wrong
- frustration, which could lead to aggression
- somatic anxiety (thinking that we are anxious can lead to physiological symptoms)

If athletes can focus their attention on the correct cues, cognitive anxiety will decline at the start of a performance. If not, or if something negative happens during the performance that causes more doubt, then cognitive anxiety will persist throughout.

Somatic anxiety

Somatic anxiety is the physiological part of anxiety and is associated with arousal. As with arousal, it is proposed that there is an inverted-U relationship between somatic anxiety and performance. Somatic anxiety aids performance up to a point, but then causes performance to deteriorate. This is shown in the graph below.

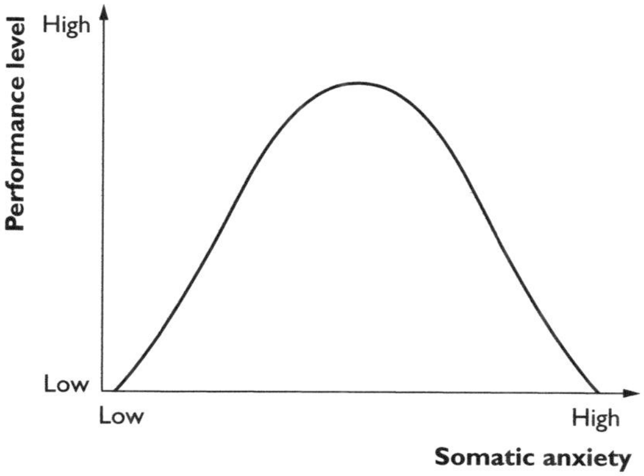

Levels of somatic anxiety fluctuate greatly. It usually declines rapidly once a performance begins.

The symptoms of somatic anxiety are often described as the 'fight-or-flight' responses. These have evolved from a time when, faced with danger, humans had to fight or flee to save their lives. The physiological changes include:

- increased heart rate (to prepare for fighting or fleeing)
- increased rate of breathing (to prepare for fighting or fleeing)
- starting to sweat (in anticipation of the need to regulate an increase in temperature)
- an increase in blood pressure (to increase the amount of oxygen travelling to the muscles to aid fighting or fleeing)
- an increase in the release of fibrinogen (blood clotting agent, to reduce bleeding to death)
- an increase in muscular tension (to prepare for fighting or fleeing)

- the need to go to the toilet (making a person lighter for running away!)
- reduced blood flow to the organs and digestive system in order to supply the muscles (the feeling of 'butterflies' in the stomach)

Facilitative (positive) anxiety

Recent research has questioned whether some anxiety can be positive. For example, it might be good to be *concerned* about an upcoming competition because it focuses attention on the task in hand. Some athletes like the feeling of excitement before a game — but is this anxiety? There has been research into **facilitative anxiety**, in which some questionnaires have asked for the 'direction' of anxiety — does the performer think that those thoughts or feelings are positive or negative?

Some researchers disagree, and think that excitement and concern are different from anxiety. They suggest that anxiety is always negative.

Measuring anxiety

The methods used to measure motivation also apply here. Interview and observation can be used, although they are time consuming and the results are often difficult to interpret. Questionnaires are often used. There are a number of validated questionnaires to measure trait and state anxiety.

The Sport Competition Anxiety Test (SCAT, Martens, 1977) measures trait anxiety. The Competitive State Anxiety Inventory-2 (CSAI-2, Martens et al., 1990) measures state anxiety. The latter is based on the multidimensional anxiety theory and has constructs to measure cognitive anxiety, somatic anxiety and self-confidence. Generally, if people have high self-confidence, they have low cognitive anxiety, and vice versa.

Biofeedback is another way of measuring arousal and somatic anxiety. This technique uses biological information to work out arousal levels. The most basic example is measuring a pulse. **Heart rate monitors** make this task a little easier. Arousal levels can also be found by using **galvanic skin response** monitors. These measure sweat, usually on the fingers, and are very sensitive.

Coping with anxiety

Everybody suffers from anxiety at times. In sport, where there are winners and losers, anxiety is a frequent problem. Athletes, coaches and sports psychologists need to have a series of planned strategies that will help to prevent anxiety or to alleviate its symptoms.

Tip For any question on anxiety, you should be able to suggest four or five ways to help eliminate the problem.

The matching hypothesis suggests that cognitive anxiety should be treated with a cognitive intervention and somatic anxiety should be treated with a somatic intervention. However, other researchers have suggested that all anxiety starts in the mind and that some form of cognitive intervention should be used for all anxiety.

Strategies for coping with anxiety include:

- **relaxation techniques or meditation** — these distract the mind away from negative thoughts because the person has to focus on relaxing (cognitive) and the relaxation eases muscular tension (somatic).
- **imagery** — since imagery starts by relaxing, anxiety should be relieved, as indicated above. Then, the process of imaging successful past and future performances should increase self-efficacy and help performers to believe in their ability (cognitive).
- **self-talk** — using a series of positive self-focused statements, which can be linked to positive mental images that reinforce the ability of performers and what they need to do in the competition, enhances self-efficacy and focuses attention (cognitive).
- **routine** — having a set routine for the build-up to a competition should help performers feel relaxed, comfortable and confident (cognitive). Knowing what they are doing and when they are doing it should limit uncertainty, which often leads to anxiety. This is a form of conditioning. Sportspeople should plan short routines for when they arrive late and lengthened routines in case they arrive at the competition early.
- **thought-stopping** — performers will recognise when a negative thought comes to mind. They should consciously stop it (cognitive) and replace it with a previously planned positive thought.
- **goal-setting** — performance and process goals that focus on the person's own performance and direct attention away from winning or losing are less likely to cause anxiety compared with outcome goals (cognitive).
- **listening to music** — this can be used to distract (cognitive) or to relax (somatic). The type of music is personal and something that relaxes one person might not relax another.
- **biofeedback** — this can be used as an early warning system for anxiety (somatic). As soon as an increase is evident, the person can focus on relaxing. Sometimes, people who use positive self-talk and other cognitive strategies can think that they are calm, but biofeedback monitors may tell a different story. Usually, when made aware of the problem, they can reduce arousal.
- **association** — the focus of attention is concentrated on certain cues associated with the performance. An example is using tunnel vision. Top sprinters are very good at this technique. Former Olympic champion Linford Christie would stand at the start line, looking down the track, focusing on what was going on in his body and seeing nothing but his lane and the finish.
- **dissociation** — attention is taken away from the competition. To prevent boredom, Paula Radcliffe uses a form of dissociation while running. She counts to 100, and back down again. The distraction is cognitive, but the form of distraction (for example, relaxation or listening to music) might also alleviate somatic symptoms.
- **worst-case scenario** — 'What's the worst that can happen? You lose, but is that so bad? It's only a game!' By reducing the importance of the event (cognitive), the notion of losing is not so fearful and the likelihood of anxiety is reduced.

- **keeping things in perspective** — there are sometimes vast amounts of money resting on a result, but a sporting competition is rarely a life-or-death situation. Recognising that there are many people in much worse positions can work to reduce the importance of the event. This is one of the reasons that footballers are often seen visiting children in hospitals. The children and parents enjoy the visits and the players put things in perspective.

Problems with anxiety research

There have been criticisms of all the anxiety theories, including the multidimensional anxiety theory. For example, the inverted-U hypothesis suggests a steady decline in performance when over-aroused, whereas a different theory suggests a catastrophic decline in performance. The newer theories (**reversal theory** and **catastrophe theory**) have different perspectives. However, they also have their weaknesses and have not been tested much in sporting environments. There is a detailed comparison and review of the multidimensional anxiety and catastrophe theories at:

www.athleticinsight.com/Vol4Iss2/Competitive_State_Anxiety.htm

The sporting environment

This part of the specification is concerned with the effect on performance of:

- people watching or evaluating
- playing at home or away

It also revisits leadership, which was covered in Unit 2.

Social facilitation

Social facilitation was defined by Zajonc (1965) as 'the presence of others in sporting situations which might result in either improvement or decrement in performance'.

The way that Zajonc categorised people who watch a performance is shown in the diagram below.

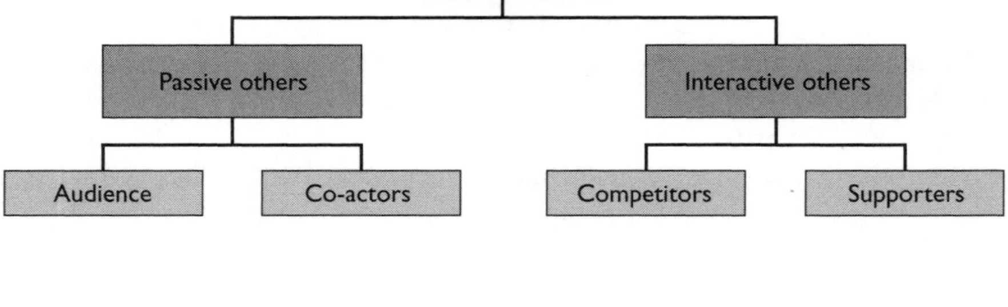

Passive others have no direct influence over performance; **interactive others** can influence performance directly.

Zajonc found that the presence of others enhanced the performance of some people and lowered the performance of others. He suggested that the presence of others increases arousal. Relating this to **drive theory**, Zajonc proposed that the higher the level of arousal, the greater the likelihood of people reverting to their **dominant response**. This can be positive or negative — for example, if the dominant response of a tennis player is a sliced backhand, this is the shot that will be performed under pressure, even when the situation needs a more attacking shot. The dominant response for elite performers should be the correct action for that situation, while lack of experience means that learners might have incorrect dominant responses.

Social facilitation theory also suggests that the presence of others will aid the performance of a simple skill and hinder the performance of a difficult skill. When a task is simple, arousal is normally low. The presence of others increases arousal so that it becomes closer to the optimum level. For more difficult skills, the arousal level is already relatively high. The presence of others will take arousal beyond the optimum level and performance will deteriorate.

Cottrell's evaluation–apprehension theory

Cottrell (1968) found some problems with Zajonc's theory. For example, what happens to arousal if people think they are being watched, but aren't actually being watched? Answer — arousal still increases. What happens if people do not know that they are being watched? Answer — no change to arousal. Cottrell had a sample of people complete a task and then repeat it with an audience. Arousal increased in the presence of the audience. He then blindfolded the audience and arousal decreased.

The **evaluation–apprehension theory** suggests that it is the fear of being evaluated by others, rather than the presence of others, that influences arousal. The perceived status of the observer would influence the strength of the increase in arousal — for example, the arousal level of a school footballer would increase more when watched by Sven Goran-Eriksson compared with being watched by his or her 6-year-old neighbour.

Coaching and teaching with social facilitation in mind

Coaches and teachers need to consider the evaluation–apprehension theory when helping people to develop their skills.

Beginners

- Learners need to be coached either individually or in small groups to reduce the fear of evaluation.
- Learners in the group should be at a similar level.
- No learner should be forced to demonstrate, unless they can perform the skill well.
- The teacher or coach must be positive in evaluating performance.

Advanced learners

- Advanced learners should be able to perform in front of others without being negatively influenced.
- Exposing advanced learners to evaluation is simulating competition and should be encouraged.
- Teaching and coaching need to include information on how to perform in front of audiences.
- Teaching and coaching should introduce information on how to perform more complex skills in front of spectators and how to cope with a demanding or hostile audience.

Home-field advantage

Home-field advantage refers to 'the consistent finding that home teams in sport competitions win over 50% of games played under a balanced home and away schedule' (Courneya & Carron, 1992). The table below shows the results of the research in this area up to 1995:

Sport	Home wins (%)
American football	57.3
Baseball	53.5
Basketball	64.4
Football	64.5
Ice hockey	61.1

Performers in the Olympics also demonstrate the home-advantage effect. Home countries consistently win two or three times more medals compared with Olympic Games played in other countries. Of the 18 countries to host the summer Olympic Games prior to 2004, 15 won their greatest percentage of available medals at home.

The exact reasons for these phenomena are unknown, but suggestions include:

- **crowd effect** — this is more apparent in the USA (NFL, NBA, NHL, MLB), and for global games such as the football World Cup and the Olympics, where teams (and therefore supporters) have to travel long distances
- **travel factors** — this effect is believed to be greater when travelling over long distances and crossing time zones
- **familiarity** — some sports have different size playing fields or even different types of surface. The home team has a better knowledge of the venue. This can prompt a more positive mood, less anxiety, better attentional focus and more control over a pre-competition routine.
- **officiating** — while it is not intentional on the referee's part, there is evidence from football to suggest that the crowd can (and sometimes does) influence decisions. This is not conclusive and officiating bodies would dispute the findings.

Leadership

In Unit 2 you learned about leadership and how it influences the learning of skills. This section focuses on how leadership can influence performance.

Leadership is 'the behavioural process of influencing individuals and groups towards set goals' (Barrow, 1977). There are many different leaders in sport — for example, managers, coaches, captains, veteran players, directors, owners, selectors and administrators.

Leadership characteristics

Leaders need certain qualities to be successful. If you are asked a question related to this, think of the qualities of the most effective leader you know. You should end up with a list along the following lines:

- knowledgeable
- assertive
- intrinsically motivated
- ambitious
- confident
- optimistic
- empathetic
- flexible
- a good communicator
- respected

Styles of leadership

Leaders can be **democratic** or **autocratic** and they can be **person-orientated** or **task-orientated**. The situation and the people who are being coached influence the style of leadership.

- **Autocratic leaders** make decisions and take control of a situation. They tend to be focused on the task and emphasise their personal authority. They may be dictatorial. They are most effective when there is a need for a quick decision, if the group is large or if the situation is dangerous.
- **Democratic leaders** tend to be person-orientated and take into account the opinions of others in the decision-making process.
- **Laissez-faire leadership** is quite rare in most sports. The nominated leader (if there is one) might act more as a consultant and other members of the group might take on leadership roles at different times.

Research has shown that males tend to prefer autocratic leaders and females tend to prefer democratic leaders. Team members tend to prefer autocratic leadership that is focused on the task. Performers from individual sports tend to want a more person-centred approach to coaching. They like to have some input in the decision-making process (democratic). Experienced and elite performers also like to have some input at times, because they often believe their previous experiences can help other group members.

The adopted style of coaching might take into account the size of the group, the number of assistants, the type of activity and any tradition associated with the activity or organisation (e.g. some football clubs want a leader who will promote a certain style of play). The age, personality characteristics and ability level of the learners might also influence the style of coaching that is used.

Leadership theories

Fiedler's contingency theory

Fiedler's theory (1978) says that leadership effectiveness depends on both the leader and the situation. He suggested that certain styles are effective in one situation and ineffective in others. Specifically, if things are going very well or badly, leaders should be task-oriented. If things are going moderately well, they should be person-orientated. Although there are flaws in the theory, it is important because it sparked debate and led to the development of other theories, such as Chelladurai's leadership model. Fiedler was the first to differentiate between task-oriented and person-oriented leaders, and to show that selecting the required style of leadership influences the success of the group.

Chelladurai's multidimensional model of leadership

Chelladurai's model shows how the coach, athlete and situation interact to influence performance and satisfaction.

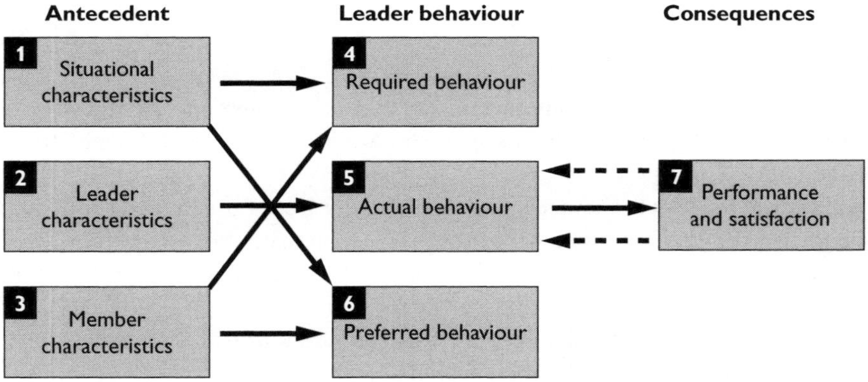

The model proposes that there is no one set of characteristics that will guarantee success. It shows that leadership styles can be changed and that effective leaders adapt to match the needs of the situation and the group members. To achieve optimal performance and satisfaction, the leader's required, preferred and actual behaviours have to be the same.

Consider the example of a relatively inexperienced football team in a district cup final, which is drawing towards the end of regulation time. There are only a few minutes before extra time begins. The players will probably want an autocratic, task-orientated style of leadership, with the team manager giving a few clear instructions that will lead the team to victory. If the manager adopts a more democratic style and starts to ask players what they think they did well and where they think they can improve (as is common in youth football), he or she might not have time to make the coaching points needed to win the game. Although this democratic approach might have been successful in the past, and might be the manager's preferred style, it would not match the needs of the specific situation.

Questions & Answers

This section of the guide has six questions covering Section B, Option B of **Unit 6: Scientific Principles of Exercise and Performance**. Each question is in the style of the examination and is worth 25 marks. The questions are broken down into sub-questions, covering a range of topics. They are based on the information included in the Content Guidance section.

When attempting to answer these questions, you should allow 30 minutes for each one. Try to use the 'define, theory, example' process for most questions. If you define the construct, then you (and the examiner) will know exactly what you are talking about. Most questions refer to one of the theories that you have studied and you will need to be able to explain this clearly. Always give a sporting example. Knowledge of theories is no use to coaches, players and sports psychologists unless they know how to apply those ideas to a sporting situation. Remember that 25% of the marks are available for the ability to apply the information in a practical context. Some questions ask specifically for an answer in terms of a sporting example. In these cases, be aware that if you fail to do so, you might not score any marks for that question, even if the information you have given is correct.

Attempt each question before comparing your answers with those of Candidates A and B.

Examiner's comments

All the candidate responses are followed by examiner's comments. These are preceded by the icon *e* and indicate where credit is due. In the weaker answers, they point out areas for improvement, specific problems and common errors, such as lack of clarity, weak or non-existent development, irrelevance, misinterpretation of the question and mistaken meanings of terms.

Question 1

(a) (i) Eysenck identified two dimensions of personality. Name these dimensions and identify a characteristic associated with each. (4 marks)

(ii) Outline the trait theory of personality and comment upon its drawbacks. (5 marks)

(iii) Many tests have been developed to assess personality. Outline one method of personality assessment, highlighting its drawbacks. (5 marks)

(b) Cottrell identified evaluation–apprehension as a factor influencing performance. Discuss the effects it may have on performance. (3 marks)

(c) (i) Using sporting examples, explain the differences between state and trait anxiety. (4 marks)

(ii) Outline the strategies that a coach may use to help an athlete cope with high levels of anxiety. (4 marks)

Total: 25 marks

Answer to Question 1: Candidate A

(a) (i) Extroversion and introversion. Extroverts are people who have outgoing characteristics ✓. They are very sociable, loud and sometimes erratic. Introverts are people who are quiet, humble and often shy ✓.

e This answer is worth 2 marks. The candidate has identified only one dimension, whereas the question asked for both. The other dimension is stable–neurotic.

(a) (ii) A trait is an underlying, enduring predisposition ✓ to respond in a certain way when a given situation occurs ✓. This theory suggests that the way people behave is governed by their genetic make up ✓ — that personality and other characteristics are passed down from the parents.

Drawbacks with this theory are that it dismisses the roles played by the environment ✓, interaction with people (society/friends) and social learning (modelling) in shaping personality ✓.

e This answer scores all 5 marks. The candidate has given a good definition of a trait, described some of the theory and identified two of the main drawbacks.

(a) (iii) Questionnaires, e.g. Cattell's 16PF ✓.

Drawbacks are that people tend to give socially desirable answers ✓ and that it can be difficult to gain any qualitative data. Often, in-depth analysis questions cannot be explored ✓.

e Candidate A gains 3 of the 5 marks. She has given an example of a questionnaire, but has not given any details about its use. She could have said that this questionnaire measures personality traits and can be used to develop a personality profile. Marks for such questions are often awarded specifically. Here, there is 1 mark for identifying a questionnaire, 1 mark for an explanation of the questionnaire and a maximum of 3 marks for the disadvantages. If a candidate listed five disadvantages without identifying and explaining a questionnaire, only 3 marks could be awarded.

(b) Apprehension may hinder performance.

It may have an effect on performers' arousal levels and self-efficacy. It may cause them to be over- or under-aroused or to be too anxious and nervous prior to performance. Consequently, they will not be able to reach optimum performance.

This answer is not worth any marks. The candidate has little understanding of Cottrell's apprehension–evaluation theory and has guessed the answer. This is not a bad idea — if you don't know something. However, in this case, it has not been successful.

(c) (i) State anxiety is how one responds to a situation. It changes according to the situation ✓. For example, a performer might find out that the opponent in the next round of a competition is tougher than expected ✓. (Martial-arts sports, such as judo or karate, are examples of where this might happen.)

Trait anxiety is a part of one's personality that tends to view situations (sporting) as stressful. This is often a stable, regular factor as it is a trait feature ✓. For example, a striker in football might always feel very stressed before a game, be it a friendly or a cup final.

This answer is worth 3 out of 4 marks. The definitions are good, but the football example could illustrate state anxiety. If the footballer is only stressed before football matches, he or she may not have high trait anxiety — most players feel some anxiety due to increasing arousal levels.

(c) (ii)
- Relaxation techniques will reduce muscular and psychological tension and may help distract the performer from the pressures of the competition ✓.
- Imagery helps the athlete to visualise success ✓.
- Support and guidance, for example from a sports psychologist, will help.
- Setting out a structured routine before every match or competition, to enable the performer to become familiar with the proceedings, will make him or her feel more relaxed and comfortable with the surroundings ✓.

This answer scores 3 marks. The candidate has answered well, but does not gain a mark for 'using a sports psychologist'. While this might be true, it gives no specific details of a strategy that this psychologist might suggest to reduce anxiety.

Candidate A scores 16 marks out of 25, which is equivalent to a grade C.

Answer to Question 1: Candidate B

(a) (i) Eysenck's theory identified two dimensions — one going from stable to neurotic ✓ and the other from introvert to extrovert ✓. Introverts are generally quiet ✓, keep to themselves and might lack self-esteem. Extroverts are normally loud, confident and outgoing ✓ people. Stable describes people who do not change much in terms of their emotional state ✓. Neurotic people can switch from being calm to being excited or angry very quickly ✓. Pete Sampras is an example of a stable introvert and Roy Keane is an example of a neurotic extrovert.

This answer scores the full 4 marks. The candidate has made six points worthy of marks, although only 4 marks are available. The different dimensions of the theory are identified and examples of characteristics are given. The candidate demonstrates understanding by also giving examples from sport. While this is not required, it does indicate the level of understanding. It might earn a mark if the examiner were unsure of what the candidate meant in another part of the answer.

(a) (ii) A trait is a general, underlying, enduring ✓ predisposition to behave in a certain way each time a given situation occurs. Traits are inherited ✓ from our parents. Traits can be identified through questionnaires and other methods of assessment, which means that behaviour can be predicted ✓. For example, if people have high trait motivation, the theory says that they will be very motivated in all that they do. A drawback of trait theory is that behaviour cannot be correctly predicted in all situations ✓. The theory does not take into account the influence of the situation ✓ on behaviour or the influence of socially learnt ✓ behaviour. For example, a PE student might not be motivated in one sport, but be very motivated in another.

This answer scores all 5 marks. A good definition of a trait is given, together with some points from the theory. The candidate has made six points worthy of marks, although only 5 marks are available. If you have time, it is a good idea to try to make an extra point in case one of your others is wrong.

(a) (iii) Questionnaires ✓ (such as Eysenck's EPQ ✓) can be used to measure personality traits and to identify what sort of traits a person has ✓. The EPQ measures introvert–extrovert and stability–neuroticism. One drawback of using a questionnaire is that sometimes people do not give honest answers ✓. Instead, they might give socially desirable answers. The questionnaire might not be reliable or might not be valid for the sample — for example, if an adult version of a questionnaire were given to children ✓. Some questionnaires are culturally specific. For example, the 16PF was developed in the 1940s and asks: 'do you prefer big band music or marching band music?' This is not relevant to most people today ✓. Also, questionnaires cannot follow up an interesting point to examine it in more depth, in the way that an interview can ✓.

This is a very good answer, making seven correct points and scoring all 5 marks. The candidate has identified a drawback and then given an explanation, to make sure that the examiner understands what he is trying to say.

(b) Evaluation apprehension is when people feel that someone is watching and judging ✓ their performance, and this increases their arousal. The inverted-U theory shows that increasing arousal can improve or worsen performance, depending on the initial level of arousal. If arousal is below the optimum level, evaluation apprehension will improve performance. If it is at or above the optimum level, then performance will get worse as arousal goes even higher. Beginners tend to have high arousal, so when they think they are being judged, arousal often goes beyond the optimum point and performance gets worse ✓. Experts often have arousal below their optimum levels, so when they think they are being judged, their arousal increases and becomes closer to the optimum, so they perform better ✓.

This answer gains all 3 marks. The candidate has followed the process of 'define, theory, example'. Although some of the theory points are not rewarded with marks, this step-by-step process makes sure the candidate gets the information across.

(c) (i) Trait anxiety is a general, underlying, enduring predisposition to be anxious ✓. This means the person would be anxious in most situations, even when most people would not be worried. Trait anxiety could be shown, for example, by a footballer who worries about not being picked when he or she has started every game of the season ✓ or who worries about a game a week before, when most people only start to be nervous a couple of days before.

State anxiety is being anxious at a certain time and it changes from moment to moment ✓. A person can feel nervous about one thing but not about another. For example, the footballer might not be nervous during the game, but when it comes to his or her penalty in the penalty shoot-out of the cup final, nerves might prevail ✓.

This question is quite straightforward. Generally, candidates answer this type of question well, as demonstrated here. Candidate B scores all 4 marks.

(c) (ii) Teaching relaxation techniques ✓, such as progressive muscular relaxation, would help to reduce cognitive and somatic anxiety. Using imagery ✓ would help the athlete to relax and to focus on what needs to be done. It can reduce cognitive and somatic anxiety. The athlete could use a distraction strategy ✓, such as listening to music. The coach could set goals that the athlete would be confident of achieving, so that the athlete becomes less cognitively anxious. For example, rather than saying the athlete needs to win, the coach could set a goal of running a certain time ✓. The athlete could self-talk ✓, using certain planned phrases that highlight what he or she can do well. This would help to keep the athlete focused.

This answer is worth the full 4 marks. Again, the candidate has made one more point than is required, just to make sure. If time were short, he could have earned the marks by using bullet points. For example:

- relaxation techniques, such as meditation
- imagery
- distraction strategy, such as listening to music
- setting 'smarter' goals, to focus on performance and not outcome
- self-talk, focusing on positive points

Candidate B scores all 25 marks, which would be grade A.

Question 2

(a) (i) Outline the psychoanalytic theory of personality, identifying its drawbacks. (3 marks)

(ii) Identify why many psychologists prefer the interactionist theory of personality. (3 marks)

(b) (i) Using sporting examples, describe *two* causes of aggression in sport. (2 marks)

(ii) Discuss the view that aggressive behaviour can be either a learned or an instinctive response. (4 marks)

(iii) Identify strategies that aggressive players could employ to control aggression. (3 marks)

(c) (i) Using examples from sport, identify the factors that may lead to learned helplessness. (2 marks)

(ii) Identify ways in which a coach may limit the effects of learned helplessness. (4 marks)

(d) Individuals approach competition or sport differently. Explain the differences between those who *need to achieve* and those who *need to avoid failure*. (4 marks)

Total: 25 marks

Answer to Question 2: Candidate A

(a) (i) This is an outdated theory suggested by Sigmund Freud. It consists of three elements ✓: id, ego and superego ✓.

e There is a maximum of 2 marks for outlining the theory and a maximum of 2 marks for the drawbacks. Here, the candidate can only be awarded 2 marks because he has not identified any drawbacks. He should at least have had a guess.

(a) (ii) Generally, they believe that behaviour is a function of both personality and the environment ✓. This theory encompasses the role that interaction with others and the environment plays in personality, while attributing some features of personality to the trait concept ✓, i.e. we behave in certain ways because it has been genetically passed down to us to act or respond in that fashion.

e This answer is also worth 2 marks. The candidate has given a definition and some of the theory. He could have said that this theory explains why different people react differently in the same situation and why a particular person will react differently in different situations. If he had followed the 'define, theory, example' process, he could have picked up the third mark from the example. He could have used Andre Agassi, who is quiet and humble off the tennis court but on court is an outgoing, confident showman.

(b) (i) Deliberate prevention of a goal being attained by an opponent — for example, a defender in football deliberately committing a professional foul against an attacker who had a clear goal-scoring opportunity ✓.

Unjust officiating — for example, an umpire in tennis ruling a shot out when it was clearly in. The American tennis player John McEnroe often demonstrated acts of aggression when the umpire overruled some of his shots.

This answer is worth 1 mark. Although the candidate has given two parts to the answer, both scenarios would cause frustration, which would be the actual cause of aggression. Again, if he had followed the 'define, theory, example' process, he would have picked up the second mark. This answer refers to the frustration–aggression hypothesis. The candidate could have looked to ethological theory (fight for survival, defence of territory, cathartic effect of sport), trait theory (an innate need to be aggressive) or social learning theory (behaviour learned from others) for another cause of aggression. Note that two of these theories are referred to in the next part of the question! By reading all the questions before starting to write, you can sometimes pick up clues to some of the answers.

(b) (ii) Learned aggression is aligned with the social learning theory of aggression. This proposes that aggressive behaviour is learned through observation, modelling and positive reinforcement ✓. If performers have previously witnessed someone get away with an aggressive act without punishment (and perhaps even being praised for it), they may decide to copy that aggressive act if the situation lends itself ✓.

Instinctive response is aligned with the instinct theories of aggression, i.e. that it is emotionally driven and that humans have the same aggressive nature and fundamental aggressive tendencies as other animals ✓.

I feel in some ways that aggression is instinctive, depending on the situation. Often aggression needs to be expressed and sport provides the opportunity for that. However, I feel that, like all things in life, we learn and observe from others. Therefore, I feel that most aggression expressed on the sports field is learned, as there may be a possible reward or benefit, e.g. intimidation of an opponent.

This answer gains 3 marks out of 4. The first part of the answer is good. The candidate has based the answer on the two theories and has shown some understanding of them. The question asks the candidate to 'discuss' the two viewpoints and does not offer marks for drawing conclusions. The last paragraph cannot earn any marks.

(b) (iii)
- The social learning theory could be employed, because performers can learn to respond in a non-aggressive manner and reinforcing this will increase the likelihood of it occurring ✓.
- Employ a sports psychologist.
- Learn relaxation cues for when feeling frustrated ✓.

The candidate has suggested the use of a sports psychologist. However, this would be an indirect strategy, so he scores only 2 marks out of 3. The candidate should be able to offer enough direct strategies to pick up all 3 marks. For example, he could have included cognitive strategies (count to 10), distraction strategies, avoiding aggressive situations (walk away), considering the consequences (fines, bans etc.) or channelling aggression in another way.

(c) (i) Attributing failure to internal and stable factors may lead to learned helplessness — for example, concepts such as 'we lost because we are not good enough'. Factors such as low self-esteem and low motivational drive and self-efficacy may lead to learned helplessness.

The theory is correct, but the question asks for examples from sport. The candidate has not given such examples, so no marks can be awarded. Note that this is a common requirement for this exam. If you do not give sporting examples, you risk getting no marks, even if it is evident that you know what you are talking about.

(c) (ii)
- Make performers attribute failure to external and unstable factors ✓.
- Use motivational tools to increase the motivational drive of the performers prior to performance.
- Assure performers of their ability pre- and post-performance to help to increase self-efficacy ✓.
- Take the positive factors out of a failure and build upon them ✓.

This answer is worth 3 marks. Time is obviously short and the candidate has started to answer using bullet points. While this is not ideal, if time is short it is a good way to get some points down quickly to earn marks. The point about motivational tools is too vague to score.

(d) Those who have a high nAch:
- are challenged and motivated by difficult situations ✓
- persist in times of difficulty ✓
- take value in success because they have worked hard for it ✓
- take positives from failure ✓

Those who have a naF:
- have low expectations
- enjoy small challenges
- have a fear of failure
- are shy and stay away from competition or challenging situations ✓

This answer scores 3 marks. There are 2 marks available for the 'need to achieve' constructs and 2 marks for the 'need to avoid failure' ones. The candidate makes four points in the first part that are worthy of marks, but can only score a maximum of 2. In the second part, there is only one point worthy of a mark. The other responses are along the right lines, but need further explanation to convince the examiner that the candidate knows what he is talking about.

Candidate A scores 16 marks, which would be grade C.

Answer to Question 2: Candidate B

(a) (i) The psychoanalytic theory was developed by Freud and is based on the id, ego, and superego ✓. These control our inner desires by assessing what we 'want' against morals and conscience, and our behaviour is usually a compromise ✓. The theory is based on Freud's case studies, so the research cannot be generalised ✓ in the way that the trait and social learning theories can. Any problems are usually related to traumas in childhood or adolescence. This does not relate very well to sporting situations, so this approach is not studied or used much in sports psychology.

e This is a difficult question because the psychoanalytic theory is rarely used in sport. However, the candidate shows an understanding of the theory and the problems associated with it in terms of sports psychology. She scores all 3 marks.

(a) (ii) The interactionist theory combines trait theory ✓ with the situation and, therefore, also includes social learning aspects ✓. It says that behaviour is a function of the personality and the environment — $B = f(P,E)$ ✓. People prefer this theory because it takes into account that we have genetic traits, for which there is a lot of evidence, and that we change our behaviour in certain situations ✓, for which there is also evidence.

e This answer is worth all 3 marks. This is an easier question, as the interactionist theory is more common than the psychoanalytic theory. As with Candidate A, this candidate could have explained that the theory explains why people react differently in different situations and why people of similar traits react differently from each other in the same situation.

(b) (i) Aggression is a behaviour in which there is intention to cause physical or psychological harm to another human being. Social learning theory ✓ says that we will act aggressively if we have modelled our behaviour on someone who we have seen being aggressive. For example, a young netball player could see a more experienced player being aggressive, gaining advantage from the behaviour and not being punished for it ✓. In a similar situation, the young player might copy the older player. The aggressive cue theory says that frustration ✓ increases the likelihood of aggressive behaviour. For example, a player whose team is losing and who is not playing very well might become frustrated and then hit someone ✓.

e Candidate B scores both marks. Despite there only being 2 marks available, she has followed the 'define, theory, example' process. She has given a good definition and then used the theories to guide her answer and supported points with examples. Compare this answer with that of Candidate A.

(b) (ii) The ethological theory says that, like other animals, humans are aggressive and have a genetic need ✓ to be aggressive. In animals, aggression is needed to defend territories or to fight for survival. Humans normally do not have to do this and so have to satisfy their aggressive needs in other ways ✓. Sport is one way they can let off steam. Other people think that aggression is instinctive in people who have high trait aggression. However, social learning theory has shown that aggressive behaviour can be learned from significant others ✓. Albert Bandura showed this in his 'bobo' doll experiment, in which children copied their parents who had been aggressive.

This answer is worth 3 marks out of 4. The first part of the answer is good, but when talking about social learning theory, reinforcement has not been mentioned. Remember that when you refer to this theory, the key words are *modelling* and *reinforcement*. If the aggressive behaviour had been punished, it would not have been copied. If it was unpunished or praised, it would have been more likely to be copied.

(b) (iii) Aggressive players could use relaxation techniques ✓ to calm themselves down. They could use self-talk ✓, to help them to focus on what they need to do and to stop them being distracted. They could be punished very heavily for aggressive behaviour and, if they are aggressive, they should be reminded of the consequences ✓. They could use imagery ✓ to help them practise what to do when they feel frustration building up or when they think they might be aggressive.

Having covered aggression theory in the previous two question parts, there is no need to go back over definitions and theories here. The candidate simply lists and explains four techniques that can help reduce aggressive behaviour. Four good points have been made in response to a 3-mark question.

(c) (i) Learned helplessness is when a person expects to fail because he/she has experienced failure many times before and has attributed it to internal and stable factors ✓, such as lack of ability. For example, if a girl has tried high jump but always knocks the bar off, she will come to think that she simply cannot do it, no matter how low the bar is. This might then transfer to other events involving jumping, such as the triple jump or hurdles. She could then go on to think that she is no good at athletics and, perhaps, all sports ✓.

Although this question is only worth 2 marks, the candidate needed to be thorough with her answer. This is lucky — the second mark was not awarded until the last sentence. Other relevant points include attributing failure to uncontrollable factors (e.g. 'I'm no good at basketball because I'm too small') or the fact that people with learned helplessness have low self-efficacy.

(c) (ii) A coach needs to give the person some success. This could involve setting small and achievable goals ✓, then, as the person has a little bit of success and starts to feel more positive, the goals are made a little bit harder. Coaches could tell people with learned helplessness what they can do well and show them that they have positive attributes ✓. They could attribute any failure to external or unstable factors ✓ — for example, 'You failed because you made a technical mistake, but that can be corrected easily' or 'You failed because you stopped concentrating. Make sure you stay focused next time'.

This is a good answer, gaining 3 of the 4 marks. To score the fourth mark, the candidate needed to say that the coach should attribute any success to internal and stable factors.

(d) People with high need to achieve are driven by difficult challenges ✓. They are highly motivated, and are not put off by occasional failure ✓. People who need to avoid failure will not take part in an activity if they think they might lose. They do not want to experience the shame and humiliation of losing ✓. In sport, this means that they will only take part if they know that they will win — for example, an adult playing tennis against his 7-year-old niece. Sometimes, they will take part when they know they can't win, but only if no-one expects them to ✓. For example, they might play tennis against Roger Federer because there would be no shame in losing to him.

This is a well-answered question, scoring all 4 marks.

Candidate B scores 23 marks, which would be grade A.

Question 3

(a) Describe the *associative* theory of learning and apply it to a sport of your choice. (4 marks)
(b) How do the three layers of personality outlined by Hollander influence behaviour? (3 marks)
(c) Using attribution theory, discuss what a coach would say to a team that has played well but lost. (5 marks)
(d) Bandura suggested that self-efficacy is influenced by four factors. Identify and apply these factors to a sport of your choice. (4 marks)
(e) Fiedler's contingency model suggests that the effectiveness of a leader can change, depending on the situation. Use sporting examples to explain this theory. (4 marks)
(f) With references to sporting performance, explain how cognitive and somatic anxieties differ. (5 marks)

Total: 25 marks

■ ■ ■

Answer to Question 3: Candidate A

(a) It is the theory that a stimulus leads to a particular response. The idea is that learning strengthens the bond ✓ between the stimulus and the response ✓. In table tennis, the stimulus might be recognising the spin on the ball and the response would be to play with the right return ✓. If the player makes the wrong choice, then the ball is unlikely to be returned. For example, if the first player puts back-spin on the ball and the second player tries to top-spin the return, the ball will probably not clear the net.

This answer is worth 3 marks. The candidate has shown a basic understanding of the associative theory (strengthening the S–R bond) and given a good example. However, more detail of the theory is needed to score all 4 marks. If you know who developed the theory, or the experiments that were carried out, you should mention this. To describe the associative theory of learning, you should outline the work of Pavlov or Skinner, to show how they demonstrated strengthening the stimulus–response bond.

(b) The inner layer is the core of the personality that we don't reveal to many people. The next layer is the typical behaviour layer. This is how we behave generally. For example, if we are funny and outgoing, then we will be funny and outgoing in most things we do ✓. The outer layer is the role-related layer. For example, if we are normally funny and outgoing, but we are in a dangerous situation, then our behaviour will change ✓.

Candidate A earns 2 of the 3 marks. Although she has identified all three layers of personality, she has not outlined how the core layer influences behaviour.

(c) The coach would blame things like luck, the referee or the opposition ✓. He would not blame his own players because they played well. By not blaming his players, he allows them to keep their confidence and to be motivated ✓ for the next game.

This is a poor answer. The candidate has not written enough, or made enough points, for a 5-mark question. She has failed to show a good understanding of the theory and has not used the correct terminology. She should have referred to attributing the loss to external, unstable or uncontrollable factors, rather than just giving examples. She could have mentioned praising the players for their positive performance and attributing this to internal and stable factors. Candidate A scores 2 marks.

(d) Having done it before — for example, a high jumper who has previously jumped a certain height will be confident that he or she can do it again ✓.

Others having done it before — if the high jumper has not jumped the height, but knows that other people have, then he or she would be confident that it could be done ✓.

Verbal persuasion — telling people that they can do it will increase their self-efficacy ✓.

The candidate has identified three of the four sources, so can only score 3 marks. In this instance, she has not been penalised for not knowing the correct terminology. This is because she has given good explanations and it is clear that she knows the information. However, many candidates lose marks for using incorrect terminology and vague examples. You should know and use the appropriate words and phrases related to each theory. In answer to this question, 'performance accomplishments' and 'vicarious experiences' should have been used, as well as 'controlling emotional arousal', which was not mentioned by this candidate.

(e) The leader might need to change his or her leadership style depending on the situation. In a dangerous situation, someone who is normally a democratic leader might need to be autocratic in order to take control. An example could be in gymnastics, where the coach lets people help decide what they are going to do. However, if someone could get hurt, then the coach would have to be forceful and stop the dangerous behaviour.

This answer fails to score. The candidate has taken a basic aspect of the theory from the question, but has then answered in relation to autocratic–democratic differences in leadership style. While these are part of Fiedler's theory, they are only mentioned as characteristics of task- and person-oriented leadership styles. The answer should have focused on these styles.

(f) Cognitive anxiety is the psychological ✓ side of anxiety and somatic anxiety is the physiological ✓ side. Cognitive anxiety is having negative thoughts and worrying that you cannot do what needs to be done. If footballers are worrying, then they might not be able to concentrate on performing and are more likely to make mistakes, which makes them worry more ✓.

Somatic anxiety might be experienced by footballers before a game. They might want to go to the toilet, feel butterflies in the stomach and have fast heart rates. Somatic anxiety makes performance better up to a certain point. Past this optimum point, performance gets worse ✓.

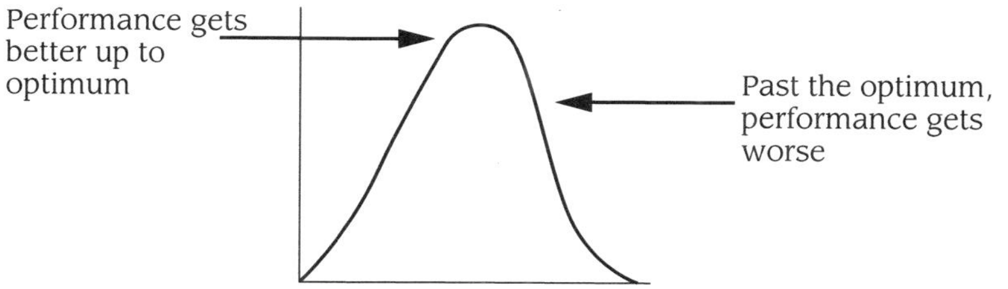
Performance gets better up to optimum
Past the optimum, performance gets worse

This is a good answer, scoring 4 marks. The candidate has given a definition of the two types of anxiety and her examples are sound. She would have gained another mark for the graph if she had labelled the axes. It is often a good idea to use diagrams and graphs to show your understanding, but you must make sure that you label everything correctly.

Candidate A scores 14 marks, which would be grade D. She demonstrated sound knowledge in places, but needed to explain the theories more clearly. If she had practised answering questions using the 'define, theory, example' process, then she would have picked up more marks.

Answer to Question 3: Candidate B

(a) The associative theory is based on a particular stimulus bringing about a particular response ✓. Skinner demonstrated in animals how behaviour can be shaped and reinforced ✓ to develop the stimulus–response bond. The aim is to make this a habitual response by repeating the S–R process to gain feedback and success, which strengthens the bond ✓. For example, in basketball, performing a set-shot correctly should increase the chances of scoring a basket ✓. Seeing the ball going through the rim reinforces the S–R bond. In the future, the person will try to do the same thing again.

This is a well-answered question, gaining all 4 marks.

(b) Hollander proposed that we have an inner psychological core. This is where our morals and attitudes are formed, which will influence performance ✓. For example, if we feel that there is never an excuse for using violence, then we are less likely to be violent in a sporting situation compared with someone whose morals are different. The second layer of personality is our typical responses — the way we normally behave in day-to-day situations. For example, a person with good leadership skills might always attempt to lead groups, whether at work or in sport ✓. The outer layer is the role-related responses layer, where people adopt a certain personality to meet the demands of the situation. For example, a normally quiet person may become an aggressive, dominating basketball player ✓.

Candidate B scores 3 marks. This is a thorough answer, demonstrating a good understanding of the theory.

(c) Weiner's theory of attribution suggests that a coach should attempt to maintain confidence and motivation ✓ by attributing the defeat to unstable ✓, external ✓ or uncontrollable causes. The coach should also try to reinforce the positive performance and attribute that to internal and stable ✓ causes. For example: 'We played well because we have good ability (internal/stable), but today we were unlucky (external/unstable). The referee made a couple of poor decisions (external/unstable). However, we maintained our concentration (internal/unstable) and never let our effort (internal/unstable) drop ✓ '. By doing this, the team will keep its confidence and will be motivated to carry on competing.

e This answer is worth the full 5 marks. The candidate has used the correct terminology, explained the theory and the consequences of using this behaviour (maintain confidence and motivation), and given a good example.

(d) Self-efficacy is a situation-specific confidence. It is influenced by previous performance accomplishments ✓. For example, if a basketball player has made free throws in the past when the game was on the line, he will be more likely to feel that he can do it again.

Vicarious experiences ✓ refer to the experiences of another person. So, although the player might not personally have made free throws when the game is on the line, he knows that it has been done before and can be confident that he can do it too.

The third factor is verbal persuasion ✓. The player might not know if anyone has done it before, but the coach and other players could remind him that he is a good shooter and tell him that he is able to do it. This will increase his self-efficacy.

The final factor is controlling emotional arousal ✓. He will probably be nervous at having to take free throws at the end of a game and high arousal could cause him to miss. If he can control the arousal, he will have higher self-efficacy.

e Candidate B scores all 4 marks. This is a very good example of the 'define, theory, example' approach to answering questions. Although the question has not asked for a definition, the candidate has written it anyway. This demonstrates to the examiner that the candidate probably knows what he is talking about and helps to reinforce a point in the answer. The candidate has used basketball as the example for the third time in this question. It is a good strategy to give examples from a sport with which you are familiar.

(e) Fiedler's contingency model says that some situations suit task-oriented styles of leadership, so if there is little time to make a decision, the leader might need to work out what the task needs and make a decision.

Task-oriented leaders are focused on the performance or on winning ✓. Person-oriented coaches are more focused on people's welfare and satisfaction than on winning ✓. Fiedler's contingency says that, for example, a football manager might have to be task-oriented on some occasions and person-oriented at other times.

e This answer is worth 2 marks. The candidate has an understanding of the theory but has failed to give a clear example. He might have used a famous example, such

as Sir Alex Ferguson, who is very focused on winning and is willing to upset players by dropping them or shouting at them if it will help the team win. This example could be contrasted with a manager of a recreational five-a-side team, whose only reasons for playing are to get together and have fun. If Sir Alex were to manage this team, he would have to adopt a different style of leadership. In the past, questions on this topic have been answered poorly — probably because it is not the most recent theory, so we tend not to study it much. Consequently, candidates have confused this theory with other leadership theories, referring to democratic–autocratic leadership styles and 'great leaders' and, therefore, failing to pick up marks. It is important to be familiar with all the theories in the specification.

(f) Cognitive anxiety means negative thoughts ✓ related to performance — for example, 'I don't think I can do this'. Somatic anxiety is the physiological ✓ component of anxiety, such as feeling butterflies in the stomach, having sweaty palms, wanting to go to the toilet, having a fast heart rate and so on.

Multidimensional anxiety theory says that cognitive anxiety has a negative linear relationship ✓ with performance. The higher cognitive anxiety is, the worse the performance. So if a basketball player is about to shoot a free throw, but is thinking negative thoughts such as, 'I can't do this' or 'I missed the last one', he will not be focusing on the free throw and the performance will be worse than if there were no negative thoughts ✓.

Somatic anxiety is said to have an inverted-U relationship with performance, which means it helps performance up to a point, but then makes performance worse ✓. So if the basketball player is feeling some somatic anxiety, he knows that the body is preparing for the task at hand and that, for example, the higher heart rate will help performance. If the somatic anxiety goes too high, then the player might become too tense, or the symptoms might become a distraction and performance will be worse ✓.

The candidate has given clear definitions, explained the theory well, and reinforced understanding with good examples, again taken from basketball. This answer scores all 5 marks.

Candidate B scores 23 marks, which would be a grade A.

Question 4

(a) Individual performers have different optimum levels of arousal. Using sporting examples, explain what can influence a performer's level of arousal. (6 marks)

(b) Describe how home-field advantage can help a team to win and how this advantage can influence one of the other psychological theories that you have studied. (4 marks)

(c) Discuss the effect that the presence of others may have on sports performance. (5 marks)

(d) Social learning theory suggests that we learn through observation. How can this theory be applied to the teaching of sport to young people? (4 marks)

(e) (i) Using examples from sport, briefly describe the difference between *aggression* and *assertion*. (2 marks)

(ii) Using examples from sport, explain the *frustration–aggression* hypothesis. (4 marks)

Total: 25 marks

Answer to Question 4: Candidate A

(a) The optimum level of arousal can be influenced by personality ✓. People who are introverts have a lower optimum level of arousal than extroverts — Michael Owen is more introverted than Alan Smith and so probably has a lower optimum level of arousal ✓.

The type of activity ✓ can also influence the optimum arousal. Someone who is taking part in a sport such as shooting or archery needs a low arousal to be at the optimum because fine motor skills are involved. Someone who plays as a rugby forward with lots of gross motor skills needs a high arousal level to be at the optimum ✓.

This answer is worth 4 of the available 6 marks. The candidate has remembered two of the factors that might influence arousal. Another possible answer is referred to in part (c) — social facilitation.

(b) Home-field advantage can help a team win because the players are more familiar with the playing area ✓. These can differ in size — for example, Highbury is a small pitch compared with many other Premier League pitches. This gives Arsenal an advantage because the team is used to playing on it. Also, Arsenal's training pitches are the same size. Other teams only play at Highbury once a year and so will not be used to it. The home team also has to travel less ✓. When people have to travel long distances, it can affect the way they play. The home team usually has more supporters, which will help the team to play better ✓.

The candidate has identified three factors that can contribute to home-field advantage, but has not related these factors to one of the psychological theories. Here, candidates need to discuss how familiarity, not having to travel far, having more supporters and so on can influence another theory from the specification. For example, candidates could discuss increasing motivation, increasing self-efficacy or decreasing anxiety. Candidate A scores 3 marks.

(c) If a performance is being watched, the performer might feel worried about this, which could make the performance worse. This is called social facilitation. It increases arousal ✓, which might go above the optimum point, resulting in a poor performance ✓. Footballers might be able to score penalties easily in training, but when playing in front of 30 000 people, they will feel more pressure and might miss.

This answer is only worth 2 of the 5 marks available. The candidate has not demonstrated a good understanding of the theory. Remember that social facilitation can also aid performance for certain performers and certain tasks. She could also have mentioned Cottrell's evaluation theory.

(d) Social learning theory says that we learn from watching and copying others. People teaching sport need to make sure that they give good demonstrations so that young people can copy them correctly ✓. Teachers should then reinforce learning by telling students what they have done well and what they need to change.

The candidate has not focused on Bandura's model of observational learning as is required by the question, and scores only 1 mark. Other valid points about general teaching practice have been made, but these cannot earn marks here.

(e) (i) Aggression involves a deliberate intent to harm someone, whereas assertion is playing hard without intent to harm ✓. When Roy Keane tried to hurt a Manchester City player deliberately in a tackle, he was being aggressive. When he tries to tackle someone fairly and is simply trying to win the ball, not to hurt the opponent, he is being assertive ✓.

This is a good answer, for 2 marks. The definitions could be more detailed, but the candidate has highlighted the fundamental difference between aggression and assertion and has given a good example.

(e) (ii) This theory states that if a goal is blocked, the person trying for that goal will become frustrated. A frustrated person is more likely to be aggressive. For example, if Patrick Vieira tries to win a header but someone pulls his shirt and stops him, then he has been stopped from achieving his goal and will be frustrated. He will be annoyed and more likely to be aggressive.

This answer fails to score. The candidate has confused the frustration–aggression hypothesis (drive theory) with the revised frustration–aggression hypothesis (aggressive cue theory). The question is not about the most recent theory. You need to be aware that questions do sometimes refer to out-dated theories. The frustration–aggression hypothesis suggests that *every* time a goal is blocked there will be aggressive behaviour, not merely an increase in the *chance* of aggressive behaviour.

Candidate A scores 12 marks, which would be grade D.

Answer to Question 4: Candidate B

(a) The type of sport ✓ can influence optimal arousal. For example, to be able to perform at a high level in snooker requires low levels of arousal, because it involves fine motor skills, whereas to perform well in weight-lifting requires high levels of arousal ✓.

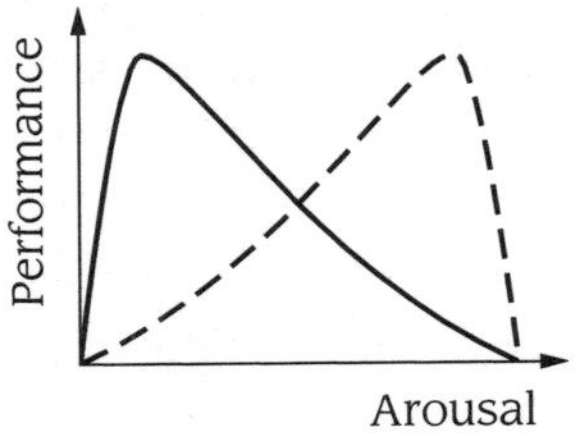

When doing the same task, learners usually have higher levels of arousal than experienced performers ✓. This is because experienced people would be more comfortable and confident in their performance, whereas the learner will be more unsure and nervous ✓.

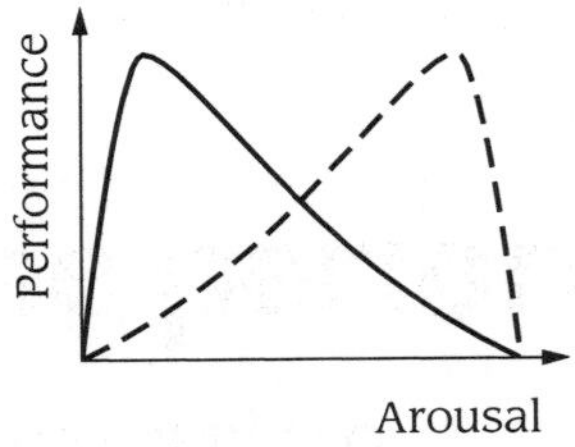

Personality ✓ influences optimum arousal. Introverts have lower optimum levels of arousal than extroverts. For example, the tennis player Pete Sampras would have a lower optimum arousal than John McEnroe ✓.

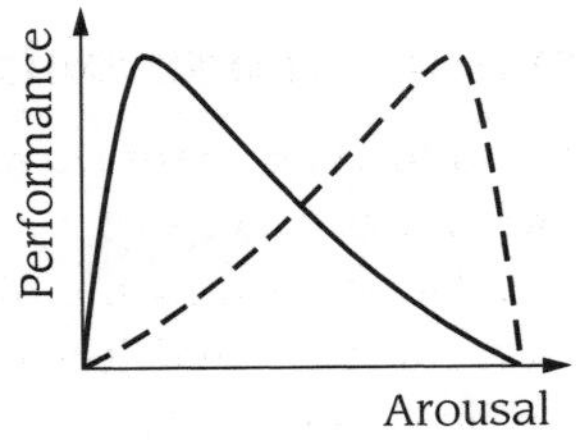

This is a very good answer, worth the full 6 marks. The candidate has given good examples and has used correctly labelled graphs to illustrate the theory.

(b) Playing at home can increase a team's confidence (self-efficacy ✓), because the players are used to the surroundings ✓ and will probably have a set routine ✓. Some teams change their tactics ✓ for home and away games, with many teams being more attacking at home and more defensive away. Referees usually give more decisions to the home team than to the away team.

Candidate B gains all 4 marks in a concise manner. The last point about referees, however, would be disputed by officials and would not earn a mark.

(c) If others are watching a performance, then they can give feedback to the performers. This means that the performers will be able to learn what they are doing wrong and this might help them to improve.

People might be more nervous about performing in front of others, compared with not having an audience, so they might not perform as well as they could. Their arousal levels could go above the optimum ✓ and they could become tense and distracted ✓ because of the pressure. Other people thrive on pressure and become even better when people are watching them.

The candidate has focused the first part of the answer on the social learning theory instead of social facilitation. Arousal has been mentioned, but the candidate does not seem to have a clear understanding of this theory. Candidate B scores just 2 marks.

(d)
- Demonstration
- Attention
- Retention
- Motivation
- Reproduction

The theory of observational learning says that young people need to be given a good demonstration ✓. (If it were not good, then they would copy a bad skill.) They need to pay attention ✓ to the demonstration and they need to retain ✓ the information. They then need to be motivated to practise ✓ until they get it right and can reproduce ✓ their version of the demonstration.

This answer gains all 4 marks. The candidate shows a good knowledge of the theory of observational learning but could have used examples to demonstrate understanding and to support the answer. Note that the candidate has written a plan. If you do this, but cross out the plan, the examiner cannot award marks. If you leave your plan, the examiner can award marks for it, should you have not reproduced the information in your answer.

(e) (i) Aggression is a behaviour in which there is intent to cause physical or psychological harm to a person. Assertion is behaving in a confident and forceful way, but with no intent to harm. In sport, aggression is usually outside the rules and assertive behaviour is playing within the rules.

Here, the candidate fails to score. The difference between aggression and assertion has been described well, but the question clearly states *'using examples from sport...'* The candidate has not used examples, so cannot be awarded any marks.

(e) (ii) The frustration–aggression hypothesis comes from drive theory and states that when players are frustrated by having a goal blocked, then they will be aggressive ✓. For example, if a hockey player is trying to dribble towards the goal but is tackled, the goal of shooting will have been blocked ✓ and the player will be aggressive, perhaps hitting out with their stick at the opponent ✓. Aggression can also be verbal. The player could shout at the defender to try to cause psychological harm.

e This answer gains 3 of the 4 marks available. The candidate has identified the correct theory and given a good example. However, the theory has not been clearly described. It suggests that *every time* a goal is blocked there will be frustration, and this will lead to aggressive behaviour.

e **Candidate B scores 19 marks, which would be a grade B.**

Question 5

(a) **Outline the principles of Bandura's self-efficacy theory and explain how a coach may use these to enhance a team's performance.** (4 marks)

(b) (i) **Using examples from sport, define and describe the autocratic, democratic and laissez-faire styles of leadership.** (6 marks)

(ii) **Using examples from sport, outline why Chelladurai's model of leadership is preferred to previous models.** (4 marks)

(c) (i) **Achievement motivation theory differentiates between two types of motivation. List these two personality types.** (2 marks)

(ii) **Motivation can be measured using questionnaires. Describe the advantages and disadvantages of using this method of data collection.** (4 marks)

(iii) **Goal-setting can be used to enhance motivation. Explain what a coach or sports psychologist needs to consider when setting goals for a performer.** (5 marks)

Total: 25 marks

Answer to Question 5: Candidate A

(a) Self-efficacy is confidence in a specific situation. A team with high self-efficacy will perform better than a team with low self-efficacy, because the players are more confident. The coach will remind them of times when have been successful in the past ✓ and will try to give them some success in training, so that they feel more confident when it comes to the competition.

The first part of the question asks for an outline of the principles of Bandura's theory. The candidate has not done this. Only 1 mark is earned, for alluding to previous performance accomplishments.

(b) (i) An autocratic leader is one who makes all the decisions and does not ask for the team's opinions ✓. An example is Roy Keane, who tells people what he thinks and takes responsibility ✓.

A democratic leader talks to the team members, listens to what they want ✓ and considers this ✓ when making decisions. An example could be the captain of a local cricket team, who listens to the players' ideas before making a decision on whether to bat first or second, who should bowl and the batting order.

Laissez-faire leadership is when there is no set leader ✓.

Candidate A scores 5 of the 6 marks available. The description of the theories is minimal, but the candidate has managed to pick up the marks. An example of laissez-faire leadership has not been given. A suitable example would be a group of runners with no set leader but who take turns to decide on the type of training they will do.

(b) (ii) Chelladurai's model is better because some people can change their style of leadership — they can be autocratic at times and democratic on other occasions.

e The candidate does not really understand Chelladurai's theory. She has had a guess and is not far away from picking up marks. However, she fails to score. Chelladurai's theory focuses on how the preferred style of leadership of the leader and the group should be the same, as well as matching the needs of the situation. This means that leaders might need to adjust their style of leadership.

(c) (i) Need to achieve (nAch) ✓

Need to avoid failure (naF) ✓

e Candidate A scores 2 marks. The question asks for a list of the personality types, so this is all that is required.

(c) (ii) The advantages of questionnaires are that they are easy ✓ to use, they can be given to many people at once and a lot of information ✓ can be obtained that would have taken a much longer time to obtain by interviews. The data are quantitative and so can be used to do statistical tests ✓. Disadvantages of questionnaires are that some people will not tell the truth ✓ and if there is something that the researcher wants to follow up in more detail, this cannot be done ✓.

e This is a good answer, which earns all 4 marks.

(c) (iii) Goals need to be 'smarter'✓. This means that they need to be:
- specific ✓ and not vague
- measurable ✓, so the person knows when the goal has been reached
- achievable ✓, because the person needs to know that it can be done
- realistic, because unrealistic goals will not motivate the person
- time-phased ✓, because there should be short-, mid- and long-term goals

e The candidate has picked up full marks here. However, a mark was not given for 'realistic' because it refers to the same point as 'achievable'. While the 'A' should be 'agreed', some people do use 'achievable'. This is fine, provided that 'agreed' is included too. The candidate did not offer 'exciting' or 'recorded', but still managed to gain the 5 marks on offer.

e **Candidate A scores 17 marks, which would be grade C.**

Answer to Question 5: Candidate B

(a) Self-efficacy is situation-specific confidence. Bandura said that there are four hierarchical sources of self-efficacy — previous performance accomplishments ✓, vicarious experiences ✓, verbal persuasion ✓ and control of negative arousal ✓. A coach can use these principles to improve the team's performance by showing the team videos of past performances ✓ in which they played well or by using imagery to picture past performances. They could watch videos of teams achieving what they need to achieve ✓. For example, if a team is going to play Manchester United, a video of Manchester United being defeated could be watched. The coach will continually give reinforcement and use verbal persuasion ✓ to suggest that the team can achieve the goal. By using some relaxation techniques ✓, the coach can also make sure that the team members are controlling their arousal levels.

This thorough answer makes eight correct points and scores all 4 marks. The candidate has followed the 'define, theory, example' process.

(b) (i) Michael Jordan was an autocratic leader. Such people are dictatorial. They take control of the situation and make decisions without the input of the group members ✓. Jordan made demands on the group with which they sometimes disagreed. However, he would stick by what he thought and would take control. He was always focused on winning and did not mind upsetting people if it meant that his team would win ✓.

Democratic leaders listen to the opinions of the group before making decisions. They are more person-orientated than autocratic leaders and are focused on the welfare of the people in the group ✓. A democratic leader might be the coach at a swimming club that has a number of experienced members, who asks what they want to do in training before planning the training schedule ✓.

Laissez-faire leadership is not very common in sport. This is when there is no structured leadership within the group and people might take on different roles at different times ✓. For example, a group of runners might train together twice a week but each time rotate the leadership roles, with a different person deciding on the type of training for each session ✓.

This answer is worth the full 6 marks. Good descriptions of the leadership styles are given, and these are supported by appropriate examples.

(b) (ii) Chelladurai's model is the preferred model of leadership because it takes into account the coach's preferred style of coaching, the actual style of coaching, the group's preferred style and the style needed by the situation ✓. Previous models focused on only parts of this model instead of bringing it all together ✓. If the coach of a football team is normally autocratic and he has young, inexperienced players who like that style, and it suits the situation, then the coach will be more effective than if there were differences in the preferences ✓.

Matching the situation to the needs can include, for example, the number in the group. If it is a small group, the leader can be democratic. For example, if a group of experienced sprinters likes to have some input, and the coach likes to be democratic, and the situation (small group) suits this, then they are more likely to be successful ✓. If the situation is dangerous, the leader might need to change style to make a quick decision and become autocratic.

This is a sound answer, earning all 4 marks.

(c) (i) Need to achieve ✓ and need to avoid failure ✓

Candidate B scores both marks.

(c) (ii) Questionnaires can be used to gather a lot of data quickly ✓ and easily ✓. These data can be compared with normative data ✓ (which show the scores that people normally get) in order to see differences. A disadvantage of questionnaires is that they sometimes do not go into enough depth ✓. Also, people may misunderstand a question ✓ and accidentally give a wrong response. They could lie or give socially desirable responses ✓.

The candidate has given more than the required two advantages and two disadvantages to earn the marks, which is a safe response in case some are not on the examination mark scheme.

(c) (iii) Goals need to be set according to 'smarter' principles ✓. These are 'specific', 'measurable', 'agreed', 'realistic', 'time-phased', 'exciting' and 'recorded'. A coach needs to make sure they are specific ✓, so that the players know exactly what they are working on. Goals need to be measurable ✓, so that the coach and players can monitor progress. They need to be agreed ✓ between the coach and players, so that they are working on aspects that need to be worked on and that the players are happy with. Goals need to be time-phased ✓ — short-term leading to mid-term, which lead to long-term. Goals need to be exciting ✓ in order to motivate, and recorded ✓, so that progress can be monitored.

In comparison with Candidate B's previous answers, this seems a little rushed. However, he has done well to get down the key terminology and shows sufficient understanding to earn all 5 marks.

Candidate B scores 25 marks, which would be grade A.

Question 6

(a) Some psychologists believe that the environment has a role to play in shaping personalities. Explain this theory using examples from sport. (5 marks)

(b) Using examples from sport, describe the inverted-U theory related to arousal. (3 marks)

(c) Social facilitation theory suggests that arousal is increased when performing in front of others. How should coaches and teachers use their understanding of this theory to make sure that they help young people to perform well? (4 marks)

(d)

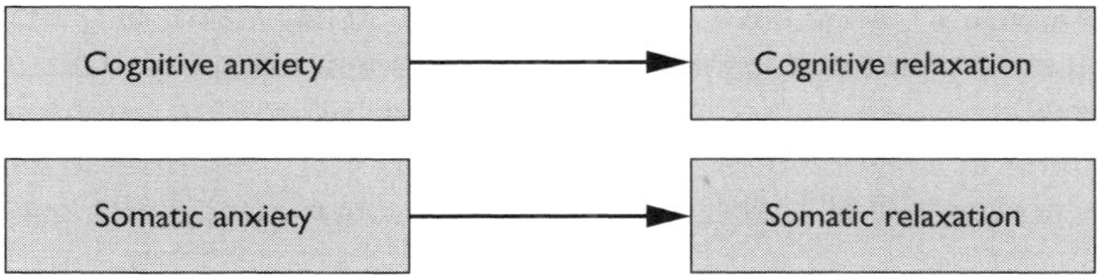

Using examples from sport, define cognitive and somatic anxiety and give examples of strategies that might be used to overcome anxiety in sport. (6 marks)

(e) (i) Identify three leadership characteristics that are important in a sports coach. (3 marks)

(ii) Autocratic and democratic styles are often used by people in leadership positions in sport. Using practical examples, explain what is meant by 'autocratic' and 'democratic' styles and identify situations in which these might be adopted. (4 marks)

Total: 25 marks

■ ■ ■

Answer to Question 6: Candidate A

(a) According to social learning theory, we learn from others by copying their behaviour ✓. If we get positive reinforcement, then we carry on with that behaviour ✓; if we get negative reinforcement, we will not repeat it ✓. If young footballers see Patrick Vieira kick someone on the pitch and get away with it, they might copy him because he is famous. If they do it in a match and get booked or sent off, then they might not do it again. However, if they get away with it or someone tells them to keep doing it, then they will carry on ✓.

e This answer scores 4 of the 5 marks available. It is a sound answer with a good example, but the candidate has not made enough points relating to the theory to earn full marks. In addition, the correct terminology has not been used. The candidate should have said 'modelling', rather than 'copying'.

(b) If I am playing football and my arousal is low, then I will be under-aroused and won't be able to play at my best. I need to be at my optimum arousal level to play to the best of my ability ✓. If I am too psyched up and become over-aroused, then I will not be able to play well.

This answer scores only 1 mark. The candidate needs to give more information about what it means to be under-aroused and over-aroused — for example, having a focus of attention that is too wide or too narrow and so missing relevant cues.

(c) Teachers need to make sure that people who are nervous when playing in front of other people feel comfortable. They can do this by making sure that they work in small groups ✓ and do not have to demonstrate. They can make sure the people in each group have similar ability ✓.

This answer is worth 2 marks. The candidate has some understanding of what is needed but has not made enough points to earn more marks.

(d) Cognitive anxiety is when a performer is anxious about the competition. Somatic anxiety is to do with the feelings of anxiety, such as butterflies and the heart rate speeding up. It can be overcome by learning relaxation-breathing techniques ✓ or by using imagery ✓.

The question says 'using examples from sport, define...'. The candidate has not given a clear definition of cognitive anxiety and neither definition is given using a sporting example. Only two strategies are given, so this answer is worth 2 marks.

(e) (i) A coach needs to be confident ✓, have a good knowledge of the sport ✓ and be positive when giving feedback ✓.

This is a concise answer, earning all 3 marks. Candidates usually get full marks for this type of question.

(e) (ii) Autocratic leaders do not ask the opinions of other people — they make decisions themselves ✓. This is good if they are doing something that is dangerous, such as teaching how to throw the discus, when it is important that people do what they are told, when they are told ✓.

Democratic leaders like to listen to what the group has to say. For example, on having to pick five penalty takers for a shoot-out, a democratic manager might ask who wants to take a penalty, before deciding on the five ✓.

This type of question is usually answered quite well. However, candidates often lose marks by not giving practical examples. This candidate has given good examples. Only 3 out of 4 marks are awarded because the definition of a democratic leader has insufficient detail.

Candidate A scores 15 marks, which would be grade C/D. The answers tend to be too brief and need more detail, particularly in relation to the theories. The theories are fundamental to answering a question correctly, since all applied psychological techniques are based on them. This candidate is lucky to score 15 marks with such weak theoretical knowledge.

Answer to Question 6: Candidate B

(a) Bandura's social learning theory proposes that people learn by modelling ✓ their behaviour on the behaviour of others. If the other people are significant others — important in the learner's life or respected highly, such as famous athletes — then they will have more of an influence ✓. Once the learner has attempted to copy the behaviour, it is reinforced ✓. This can be positive, which will increase the chances of the behaviour being repeated, or negative, which will decrease the chances of the behaviour being repeated ✓.

An example could be a young footballer watching a professional, such as Michael Owen (significant other), scoring a goal. The young player might try to copy the move that Owen made. If he scores, the goal will be positive reinforcement. Even if he fails to score, he could get positive reinforcement through praise from other players and the coach (also significant others). In this case, he will try to do the move again. If his shot goes nowhere near the goal and he is told off by the coach, then he will be less likely to repeat the behaviour ✓.

This is a good answer, scoring all 5 marks. The main terms (modelling, significant others, positive and negative reinforcement) are all included and explained well, and the example is clear.

(b) The inverted-U theory shows how arousal influences performance. If arousal is too low, people will under-perform because they will not be focused on the right cues and will miss information — for example, a netball player who does not see the person she is supposed to be marking run straight past her ✓. Optimal arousal is the point where everything is right and the player is in the zone ✓. If arousal goes over the optimum, the player becomes over-aroused and might be too tense, which could slow her down ✓.

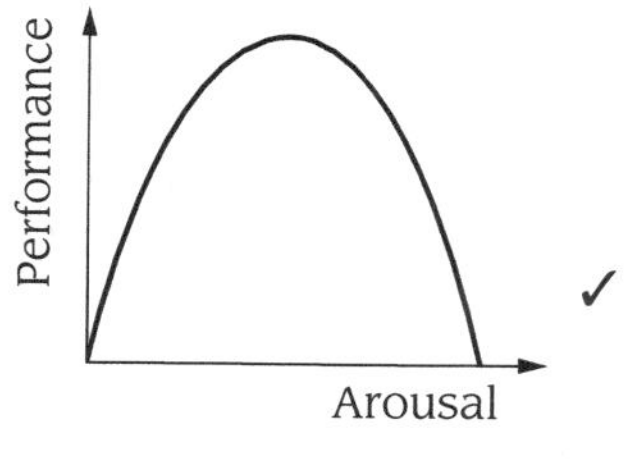

The candidate scores full marks for this question. There is a lot of information that could have been included for only 3 marks.

(c) Coaches need to make sure that the performers' arousal does not go past their optimal arousal levels ✓. They can do this by coaching them individually ✓ or in small groups ✓ of people at the same ability level ✓, so that they do not feel threatened. The coach could make sure that people only have to perform in front of the group when they can do the skill well ✓. They could also teach relaxation techniques ✓, so that when the people do have to perform in front of an audience they will be able to cope with the increase in arousal. For better performers, the coach might want to re-create the situation that they are going to face in a competition, by having them perform in front of others ✓. This is something that is done in gymnastics.

e This is an excellent answer, making seven points and scoring all 4 marks. It is clear that the candidate understands the theory. The answer gives a number of strategies for teachers and coaches to follow to help young people, ranging from beginners to more experienced performers, to perform well.

(d) Cognitive anxiety involves thoughts of not being able to complete the task successfully — for example, someone about to take a shot in netball thinking, 'I'm going to miss this' or 'I haven't practised enough' ✓. Somatic anxiety involves the physical symptoms of being nervous, such as wanting to go to the toilet, having butterflies in the stomach and sweating.

There are a lot of strategies that people can use to overcome anxiety. They could set goals that focus on performance, rather than outcome ✓. The goals should be realistic and not too difficult. Performers can learn to relax with breathing techniques that focus the mind and relax the muscles ✓. They could use imagery, which relaxes the body and focuses the mind on positive images ✓. They could use dissociation, which would involve distancing themselves from what needs to be done and not thinking about it ✓.

e This is a good answer, gaining 5 marks. The candidate lost the sixth mark because somatic anxiety is not defined in relation to a sport. This could have been as simple as adding '*before the start of a game,* wanting to go to the toilet...' When questions ask you to use examples from sport, you *must* do this.

(e) (i) Coaches need to be intrinsically motivated ✓, confident ✓, empathetic ✓ and good communicators ✓.

e Candidate B makes four correct points and scores all 3 marks.

(e) (ii) Autocratic leaders are authoritarian people who want to take the lead and make decisions for the group ✓. This style of leadership is well suited to dangerous situations, such as trampolining, in which the person in charge needs to be in control of the group for safety reasons ✓. It is also suited to coaching large groups, such as 40 students on a football camp, where it would not be practical to ask all the students what they want to do ✓.

Democratic leaders like to make the people in the group feel valued by asking their opinion and considering what the group wants ✓. This is good when working with experienced performers or with small groups. For example, if there are a couple of international players in a netball team, the coach might value their ideas and use information from them to help make decisions ✓.

e Sound definitions and good examples are given in this answer, which scores all 4 marks.

e **Candidate B scores 24 marks, which would be grade A.**